The Challenge of Urban Growth

The Challenge of Urban Growth

The Basic Economics of City Size and Structure

Niles M. Hansen
University of Texas at Austin

Lexington Books
D.C. Heath and Company
Lexington, Massachusetts
Toronto   London

Library of Congress Cataloging in Publication Data

Hansen, Niles M
  The challenge of urban growth.

  Includes bibliographical references and index.
  1. Cities and towns—United States. 2. Cities and towns—Growth. 3. Urban economics. I Title.
HT123.H34   301.36'3'0973   74-25089
ISBN 0-669-97709-8

Copyright © 1975 by D.C. Heath and Company

Reproduction in whole or in part permitted for any purpose of the United States Government.

All rights reserved. No part of this publication may be reproduced or transmitted in any form or by any means, electronic or mechanical, including photocopy, recording, or any information storage or retrieval system, without permission in writing from the publisher. The provision of the United States Government constitutes the only exception to this prohibition.

Second printing July 1976

Published simultaneously in Canada

Printed in the United States of America

International Standard Book Number: 0-669-97709-8

Library of Congress Catalog Card Number: 74-25089

Contents

	List of Figures	vii
	List of Tables	ix
	Preface	xi
Chapter 1	Introduction	1
Chapter 2	The Urban System of the United States	7
	Standard Metropolitan Statistical Areas (SMSAs)	7
	Daily Urban Systems (DUSs)	9
	Population Changes	11
Chapter 3	Where Do People Want to Live?	19
	Locational Preferences	19
	Attitudes Toward Metropolitan Growth	20
	Proximity to Metropolitan Areas	23
	Attitudes Toward Neighborhood	26
Chapter 4	Some Limitations of Economic Base and Other Models of Urban Growth	31
	Analyzing Urban Growth	31
	Economic Base Analysis	33
	Tertiary Activities	38
	Key Concepts	39
Chapter 5	Advantages of the City	41
	External Economies	41
	Innovations	42
	Income and City Size	46
	Optimum Size	48
Chapter 6	When is a Big City too Big?	49
	High Population Density	49

	Municipal Costs	52
	Per Capita Income	58
	The Size Issue	59
	Urban Growth	61
Chapter 7	**The Decline of the Central City**	63
	The Central City	63
	Employment Changes	65
	Transportation	72
	Housing	75
	Tax Policies	77
	Regional Exceptions	82
	The South	83
Chapter 8	**The Central-City Neighborhood**	87
	Affinity Environment	88
	Change in Neighborhood Composition	90
	Breakdown of Community Structure	90
	Abandonment	92
	Noncommunal Residents	94
	Government Programs	94
	Local Government Assistance	97
	The Ghetto	97
	Summary	100
Chapter 9	**The Growth Controversy in the Suburbs**	101
	Suburban Growth	101
	Effect of Tax Policies	104
	Zoning Laws	105
	Community Programs	108
	Federal and State Policies	112
	Planning and Cooperation	113
Chapter 10	**Cluster Development**	117
	Central-Place Theory	117
	Urban Structure	119
	New Towns	121
	Planned Unit Development (PUD)	123

	New-Town Goals	124
	Linear Development	125
	Clusters of Small Cities	126
Chapter 11	**Urban Growth-Center Policy and Regional Development**	129
	Growth Centers	129
	Spread and Backwash Effects	129
	Economic Development Programs	133
	Growth-Center Strategy	137
	Location Preferences	139
	Relocation Recommendations	141
Chapter 12	**Summary and Conclusions**	143
	Housing and Urban Development Act	143
	Metropolitan Growth Pressures	145
	Urban Goals	146
	Urban Problems	148
	Public Preferences	149
	Urban Policy	151
	Notes	153
	Index	169
	About the Author	175

List of Figures

2-1	The BEA Economic Areas	12
2-2	Growth Rate of the DUSs 1960-70 Related to Their Population in 1960	14
2-3	Zones of Net Inmigration, 1960-70	16
2-4	Projected Urban Regions in the Year 2000	17
6-1	Urban Cost and Product Curves with City Size	57
7-1	Per Cent of Change in Urban Population by States: 1960 to 1970	84
11-1	Economic Development Administration Development District and Growth Center Concepts	135

List of Tables

2-1	Population of the United States by Place of Residence and Race, 1950 to 1970	8
3-1	Actual Place of Residence as Described by Respondents to Population Commission Survey, 1971	20
3-2	Residential Preference of Respondents to Population Commission Survey, 1971	21
3-3	Attitudes of Respondents to Population Conmission Survey Toward Whether the Federal Government Should Discourage Growth of Large Metropolitan Areas	22
3-4	Percentage of Americans Satisfied or Dissatisfied with the Quality of Life in Their Community, 1973	28
3-5	Responses of Americans Concerning the Degree of Attractiveness of Their Neighborhood (Per Cent), 1973	28
6-1	Proportion of Americans Who Feel That They Reside Under Congested Conditions, 1973	51
6-2	The Relationship Between City Size, Population Density, and Crime Rates in United States Cities	51
6-3	Per Capita Amounts of Selected City Finance Items by Population-Size Groups, Fiscal Year 1969	54
7-1	Population Characteristics of the Twenty-five Largest SMSAs and Their Central Cities	66
7-2	Families and Unrelated Individuals Below the Poverty Level in 1972, by Place of Residence, Region and Race of Head	68
7-3	Employment Changes in 39 Selected SMSAs, Central Cities, and Suburbs, 1948, 1963, 1967	69
7-4	Employment Changes Among Civilians 14 Years and Over by Selected Nonfarm Occupation Groups 1960-70	70

7-5	Central City-Suburb Disparities for 37 Largest Metropolitan Areas in 1968	80
9-1	Areas with Growth Constraints, March 1973	102
11-1	Relative Frequency of Preferences for Home Areas, Intermediate Centers, and Large Cities, by Selected Groups of Young Persons	141

Preface

From personal observation, students, city planners, and other groups and individuals interested in the nature and significance of contemporary urban problems have been quite willing to learn what the economics profession has to contribute in this regard. Too often, however, they have been frustrated by what appear to be overly abstract arguments based on unrealistic assumptions. It must be admitted that economics professors sometimes treasure elegance more than relevance, and that hardwon intellectual capital is difficult to abandon, no matter how trivial it may be. Nevertheless, a great deal of economics is highly relevant to urban problems. The present volume, which is addressed to noneconomists, as well as to advanced undergraduate and beginning graduate economics students, is an attempt to synthesize a representative portion of this literature.

Because urban and regional economics are a relatively new field, a great deal of their content has been carried over from related areas. For example, some writers give considerable weight to public finance issues, while others emphasize transportation problems. This is not a textbook covering all such interests. Rather, it stresses those aspects of the literature that bear directly on urban growth policy. I particularly hope that it will be useful in clarifying key issues for persons—planners, government officials, students, or concerned citizens—seeking to bring positive guidance to bear on the course of future urbanization. I also hope that they will be prompted to improve on the deficiencies that remain.

I am indebted to Pamela Pape for her excellent secretarial assistance. I have also benefited from the support and counsel of my colleagues Michael Conroy, Rita Ellison, William Gruben, Eldon J. Nosari, and Koren Sherrill. The material presented here is based on work supported by an award from the National Science Foundation, to evaluate past research considered of use to policy makers at the local, state, and federal levels. The views expressed herein are those of the author and should not be attributed to NSF. The study is one in a series of 40 NSF-supported projects assessing policy research in the field of municipal systems and human resources. The other studies range from the evaluation of policy-research on the effectiveness of juvenile delinquency programs to an evaluation of research in the area of residential solid waste management. Persons interested in receiving a list describing the 40 policy-research evaluation projects should write: RANN Document Center; National Science Foundation; 1800 G Street, N.W.; Washington, D.C. 20550.

1 Introduction

This study is primarily concerned with the economics of urban growth and structure, and particularly with issues related to alternative urban growth patterns and goal choices. Although the perspective is that of an economist, the discussions are not oriented toward the theoretical interests of a relatively small number of specialists in urban and regional economics. Rather, they are intended to bridge the gap between recent policy-oriented works in these fields and the more concrete interests of city officials, planners, and students who have not necessarily acquired any significant knowledge of technical economics, but who still wish to know what contributions economics may make toward the resolution of pressing urban problems.

Urbanization is a worldwide phenomenon. Economic activities are attracted to cities because of advantages associated with concentration, and people are drawn to cities because they offer improved incomes and a diversity of career and lifestyle options. Aristotle observed that men come together in cities for security but they stay together for the good life. Although cities have never been universally regarded as places where human beings may find their greatest fulfillment, there is at present a particularly widespread sentiment that the quality of living in big cities is deteriorating. In this view, the city is associated with increasing congestion, slums, violence, welfare costs, and suburban sprawl. Whether or not there has been an actual decline in the quality of urban life, it is still legitimate to ask if it can be improved by the application of feasible public policies. The fact that this study was written and is now being read implies a probable mutual assumption that the "accidental city" can be changed for the better by the application of better planning and design. Thus, Wilfred Owen argues that:

The basic difficulty of urban growth all over the world is that decisions about the use of urban land are being made by a host of private parties without the guidance of comprehensive plans or community goals. The result is heavy social costs, which include the high costs of a bad environment and large outlays for transportation and other services needed to cope with the outcome. Transportation technology is supporting a wide variety of undesirable cities and shoddy suburbs. The only remedy is to recognize that anything is technically possible and to choose the kind of environment to be sought. The laissez-faire city is likely to end in disaster.[1]

Although technology increases the range of options available, it cannot make choices for us. It may seem that economics—which frequently is defined as the study of the allocation of scarce resources among competing uses—is especially valuable in elucidating the means for realizing urban policy objectives, for among all the social sciences it has, in fact, developed a particularly impressive apparatus for dealing rationally with alternative choices. The problem is that in spite of the discipline's credentials, it is not always helpful with respect to goal definition. Economic analysis customarily takes goals as given and then attempts to show how they can be realized in the most efficient manner. Thus, while economics often can aid decision-makers by showing the costs associated with alternative objectives, it does not pretend to establish the goals. Unfortunately, even this potentially valuable use of economics is frequently precluded by communication barriers. The language used to convey theoretical ideas tends to be abstract, conceptual, and mathematical, whereas the language of everyday planning practice tends to be concrete, discursive, and primarily verbal.

Theorists generally employ the jargon of their discipline when addressing themselves to other specialists. But practitioners may variously make use of political rhetoric, diplomatic equivocations, administrative jargon, or the language of the public information media. Most practitioners will not be schooled in the languages of science nor, for that matter, in the related processes of reasoning. This communications gap is the ultimate reason why theorists may be said to inhabit quite different worlds, and why practitioners avail themselves so little of what is known in theoretical science. The principal media of communication in the sciences, such as preprints or journals, are simply not read by those who might exact from them some practical meaning. On the other hand, the failure of practitioners to generate a demand for the products of theoretical learning contributes to making theory increasingly esoteric.[2]

While these remarks certainly are relevant to the relationship between urban and regional economics and urban planning, it is, nevertheless, true that much of the economics of spatial resource allocation has been developed in response to critical policy issues.

Wilbur Thompson noted that urban economics came into being because traditional economics, by ignoring the "where" of economic activity, lacked the spatial dimension necessary for analyzing phenomena such as suburban sprawl, dying cores, traffic tangles, and the black ghetto and the white noose, to employ vivid word pictures. Thompson also maintained that because the city is a complex system—an ecology—the greatest contribution of the economist comes "when he joins with other specialists to rationalize a broad urban system."[3]

Another prominent urban economist, Harry Richardson, has sternly protested the movement of some abstract economic theorists into the field, arguing that "it would be a disaster if a policy-oriented field such as urban economics went the way of growth theory." If this were to happen, it would, according to Richardson, "set the clock back in regard to progress in urban economics, and in several respects." The profession has progressed well beyond some of the abstract and somewhat artificial interests of a decade ago in favor of problems that are at once more complex and more important. These include:

interdependence of urban location decisions; determination of the rate of suburbanization; the development of sub-centres; problems of intraurban spatial income distribution, urban inequities and urban poverty; residential segregation by income (class, race); the causes of slums, how blight spreads and the determination of investment and social criteria for urban renewal; metropolitan fiscal problems and their implications for the provision of urban services, transportation, and slum prevention; the choice of transport modes, and investment and pricing criteria for public transport; pollution abatement and control policies; how to improve metropolitan spatial efficiency; and the development of strategies for a national urban policy. [Moreover] the key impulse to urban economic research is, and has been, the urgent policy needs of how to handle and control metropolitan cities.[4]

Similarly, a recent review of "The Development of Urban Economics in the United States" concluded that textbooks in the field "are more representative of the 1960s than of the 1970s. My guess is that increasingly over this decade, U.S. urban economists will turn their attention to new policy issues. One will be the issue of a national urban growth policy, including the question of whether to discourage the continual growth of large metropolitan centres and to decentralize the population, through, for example, the building of new towns and development of 'growth centres' in presently stagnant regions of the country."[5] This question, which I have dealt with at length elsewhere,[6] will be taken up again in Chapter 11. There is a large and growing literature concerning desirable rates of population and economic growth both nationally and in terms of individual areas. In this context the present study gives considerable attention to the trade-offs between protection of the environment and job creation; frequently, middle- and upper-class groups are the main supporters of environmental improvement, while lower-income groups are more willing to make concessions along this line if they mean more employment opportunities. Consideration of growth issues, however, must take account of the spatial organization of metropolitan areas. Many, perhaps most, urban problems are in some way related to structural differences within metropolitan areas and to the fact that rates of growth and the nature of growth differ among metropolitan communities—and particularly between the central city and suburbs.

The broad context within which urban problems and policies must be viewed is presented in the following chapter. The notion of urban policies implies that we are in some sense trying to increase the aggregate level of welfare, which in turn implies that we know something about location preferences. The limited evidence available in this regard is examined in Chapter 3. Urban growth is an extremely complex phenomenon; although existing economic models are useful for some purposes, much work remains to be done toward the development of a satisfactory general model. The scope of the present study does not permit detailed consideration of the numerous models which have been proposed. Classical location theory continues to be quite influential among regional scientists, and neoclassical growth theory appears to be increasingly in favor in some scholarly circles. I have attempted to indicate in Chapter 4 that the planner or student who does not find these approaches useful will find respectable company in academic circles. On the other hand, Chapter 4 gives considerable attention to economic base analysis because it is used so frequently by planners and perhaps even more by well-paid consultants to planning offices. In view of the relative ubiquity of this approach, it should be emphasized that it does not stand on firm ground, and I attempt to argue in some detail why this is the case. The fact that I neglect such topics as simulation, gaming, and linear, nonlinear, dynamic and stochastic programming implies no lack of respect for these types of urban analysis. Indeed, I believe that simulation techniques, if based on empirically derived assumptions, offer great promise. However, until the promise is fulfilled, a volume of this kind need not burden the reader with the technical discussions which would be required even to introduce the relevant literature.

Chapter 5 shows how proximity and external economies create advantages for firms and households in cities. The arguments explain why population and economic activities tend to concentrate in urban areas; as a corollary they also explain how big cities got to be so big. There are strong theoretical and empirical grounds for believing that big cities may be too big; these are presented in Chapter 6. Particular emphasis is given in this chapter to the need to distinguish between problems which are found in big cities and problems caused by their size as such. Many of the problems dealt with in the "urban crisis" literature are in fact amenable to resolution without placing arbitrary growth limits on big cities. However, while this point is emphasized in Chapter 6, there remain arguments against big cities which deserve serious consideration.

Chapters 7 through 10 are primarily concerned with urban structure, although it is pointed out that differing growth patterns within metropolitan areas account for a host of urban problems. Chapters 7 and 8 discuss the plight of metropolitan central cities, with the qualification that this problem is not applicable to all metropolitan areas, and particularly not to smaller metropolitan areas in the South and West. Nevertheless, it is relevant to places which account for the majority of the nation's total metropolitan population. Chapter 8 draws heavily on the work of noneconomists because economists have given very little attention to neighborhoods.

Chapters 9 and 10 are concerned with suburban problems. Millions of Americans and perhaps billions of the world's populations (without wishing to abandon their own cultural traditions in favor of the American way of life) would no doubt welcome these problems, associated as they are with economic affluence. Current community efforts to check rapid growth and to control urban sprawl are described in some detail. Although social and political motives often underlie ostensible concern for the environment, those who really want to reduce waste should give more attention to economic efficiency implications of the spatial organization of the suburbs—and indeed of total metropolitan areas.

Most of the discussions in this volume are implicitly oriented toward metropolitan areas as they exist within the current urban system, or as they are expected to develop given current trends. However, there have been calls for modifying the urban system itself. In one way or another, proponents of this approach maintain that if the spontaneous pattern of urban growth is undesirable, then efforts should be made to induce growth in alternative urban centers. The case for growth center strategies is critically examined in Chapter 11.

The concluding chapter summarizes the shifting and somewhat uncertain context within which urban and regional planning will take place in the foreseeable future. Because local situations vary considerably, it is inappropriate to prescribe blanket solutions to urban problems. Nevertheless, this should not preclude efforts to identify problems and solutions locally, though preferably within the framework of a flexible national urban growth policy which provides guidelines with respect to both social equity and economic efficiency.

While the following chapters attempt to present, in a relatively nontechnical manner, some of the insights that urban and regional economics may bring to the immediate needs of persons directly engaged in shaping our urban future, it is also hoped that these persons will be prompted to indicate areas where academic discussions are not responding to policy needs. A continuous dialogue must be maintained if the economics of spatial resource allocation is to achieve and sustain the relevance that many of us predict and hope it will have.

2 The Urban System of the United States

Before considering the economics of urban size, it is necessary to examine the nature of the national urban system. The data in Table 2-1 show that in each of the last two intercensus decades the population living in metropolitan areas grew at a faster rate than the nation's total population, though the metropolitan growth rate slowed from an annual 2.3 percent average annual increase in 1950-60 to 1.5 percent in 1960-70.

Standard Metropolitan Statistical Areas (SMSAs)

A Standard Metropolitan Statistical Area (SMSA), as defined by the Office of Management and Budget, is a county or group of contiguous counties (except in New England) that contains at least one central city of 50,000 inhabitants or more or "twin cities" with a combined population of at least 50,000. Other contiguous counties are included in an SMSA if, according to certain criteria, they are essentially metropolitan in character and are socially and economically integrated with the central city. In New England, towns and cities are used in defining SMSAs.

In 1950 the number of both blacks and whites living in central cities was considerably greater than the number living outside central cities in metropolitan areas. However, by 1960 the majority of the white metropolitan population lived in the suburbs, and in 1970 the white central city population was less than it was in 1960. In 1970, 40 per cent of the white population lived in suburban areas, compared with only 32 per cent in nonmetropolitan areas and 28 per cent in central cities. In contrast, the black population is not only more metropolitan in composition but also much more heavily concentrated in central cities. Fully 58 per cent of the nation's black population lived in central cities in 1970, whereas only 16 per cent lived in the rapidly growing suburbs. This phenomenon has been one of the principal sources of the problems dealt with in urban economics.

Table 2-1
Population of the United States by Place of Residence and Race, 1950 to 1970 (in thousands, except per cent)

Residence and Race	Population 1950	Population 1960	Population Total 1970	1970 Per Cent	Per Cent Change 1950-60	Per Cent Change 1960-70	Average Annual Change 1950-60	Average Annual Change 1960-70
Total	151,326	179,323	203,212	100.0	18.5	13.3	1.7	1.3
Standard metropolitan statistical areas	94,579	119,595	139,419	68.6	26.4	16.6	2.3	1.5
Central cities	53,696	59,947	63,797	31.4	11.6	6.4	1.1	0.6
Outside central cities	40,883	59,648	75,622	37.2	45.9	26.8	3.8	2.4
Nonmetropolitan areas	56,747	59,728	63,793	31.4	5.3	6.8	0.5	0.7
White	135,150	158,832	177,749	100.0	17.5	11.9	1.6	1.1
Standard metropolitan statistical areas	85,099	105,180	120,579	67.8	23.6	14.6	2.1	1.4
Central cities	46,791	49,440	49,430	27.8	5.7	−0.2	0.6	−0.1
Outside central cities	38,308	55,741	71,148	40.0	45.5	27.6	3.8	2.5
Nonmetropolitan areas	50,051	53,652	57,170	32.2	7.2	6.6	0.7	0.6
Black	14,972	18,792	22,580	100.0	25.5	20.2	2.3	1.9
Standard metropolitan statistical areas	8,850	12,710	16,771	74.3	43.6	32.0	3.6	2.8
Central cities	6,608	9,950	13,140	58.2	50.6	32.1	4.1	2.8
Outside central cities	2,242	2,760	3,630	16.1	23.1	31.5	2.1	2.8
Nonmetropolitan areas	6,122	6,083	5,810	25.7	−0.6	−4.5	−0.1	−0.5

Note: All figures as of April. Covers 243 SMSAs as defined in 1970.
Source: *U.S. Bureau of the Census, Statistical Abstract of the United States: 1972* (Washington, D.C.: U.S. Government Printing Office, 1972), p. 16.

Daily Urban Systems (DUSs)

In recent years, the practice of using SMSAs as units of urban analysis has been challenged on the ground that people no longer live and work in the same place, and that the separation of residence and work place continues to increase. Thus, Brian Berry has argued that:

> The commuting fields have surely become more extensive during the 1960-1970 decade. For population projections, this means that the residential areas (housing markets) related to particular employment clusters (job markets) cover zones extending far beyond both legal city limits and the boundaries of, for example, the Bureau of the Census's "Standard Metropolitan Statistical Areas," which are explicitly constructed to *exclude* all counties for which the percentage of resident workers commuting to work in the central city drops beneath 15 percent. Population projections based upon assumptions about economic activity thus need a different unit of accounting if changes in employment are to be related properly to changes in the population supported by the jobs. Such an accounting unit is the *Daily Urban System* (DUS).[1]

The Bureau of Economic Analysis, U.S. Department of Commerce, recently developed a nationally exhaustive set of regions corresponding to DUSs. These regions were defined largely on the basis of earlier commuting studies by Berry. The first step in the identification process was to select appropriate economic centers. SMSAs were chosen where possible because the SMSA center serves as a wholesale-, retail-, and labor-market focus. However, not all SMSAs were made the center of DUSs because some are integral parts of larger metropolitan complexes and have considerable cross-commuting with other metropolitan areas. For example, the New York City DUS includes not only the New York City SMSA but also the Jersey City, Newark, Patterson-Clifton-Passaic, Stamford, Norwalk, and Bridgeport SMSAs. On the other hand, in rural areas where there are no SMSAs, cities of 25,000 to 50,000 population were used as economic centers, provided that they were area wholesale trade centers and that the DUS involved would have a minimum population of about 200,000. The DUSs were defined according to the following criteria:

> After identifying economic centers, intervening counties were allocated to the centers. The assignment was made primarily on the basis of the journey to work pattern around the economic centers. Comparative time and distance of travel to the economic centers, the inter-connection between

outlying counties because of the journey to work pattern, the road network, and the linkages of counties by such other economic ties as telephone traffic, bank deposits, television viewing, newspaper circulation, and topography were also used to determine placement of peripheral counties into the appropriate economic area. In places where the commuting pattern of adjacent economic sectors overlapped, counties were included in the economic area containing the center with which there was the greatest commuting interconnection. In the case of cities where the commuting pattern overlapped to a great degree, no attempt was made to separate the two cities; instead, both were included in the same economic area.[2]

The set of DUSs thus defined are shown in Figure 2-1. Between 1960 and 1970 there were wide variations in their growth rates, but as Figure 2-2 indicates there was a clear relationship between growth and size. In Figure 2-2 the growth rate is plotted on the ordinate and 1960 population on the abscissa, using a logarithmic scale. Each dot represents one of the 173 DUSs. Horizontal lines mark a zero growth rate and the national growth rate of 13.3 per cent. The observations are grouped into roughly equal logarithmic intervals, and for each group (except for the extreme classes with the fewest observations) the median and upper and lower quartiles are shown. It is clear that the median growth rate increases progressively with size of DUS up to a population of 1,000,000 and then stabilizes at about the national growth rate. The interquartile ranges are stable up to the 1,000,000 population level; however, the upper quartile is markedly higher in the 1,000,000 to 2,250,000 size class, indicating accelerated growth of many centers in this range as they pass the 1,000,000 level. After the 2,250,000 level there is convergence again on the national growth rate. At the other extreme, it will be noted that the median growth rate is negative in the smallest size class, as is the lower quartile in the 225,000-500,000 class.

Certain broad employment pattern tendencies appear to underlie these relationships. First, the greater a DUSs dependence on primary activities, such as agriculture, the lower is its growth rate. When agriculture accounts for over 25 per cent of total earnings, there is a declining population.[3]

The second tendency involves a size-ratchet effect. Wilbur Thompson speculated that "if the growth of an urban area persists long enough to raise the area to some critical size (a quarter of a million population?), structural characteristics, such as industrial diversification, political power, huge fixed investments, a rich local market, and a steady supply of industrial leadership may almost ensure its continued growth and fully ensure against absolute decline—may, in fact, effect irreversible aggregate growth."[4] In Berry's analysis, the SMSA of 250,000 is replaced by a DUS population of at least 1,000,000. In particular, as manufacturing earnings increase, the DUS growth rate tends to stabilize around the national average growth rate.

The DUS growth rate is higher, the greater the share of local earnings derived from the tertiary sector (essentially trade and services in the broadest sense). One reason for this is the interregional migration of older people who support tertiary activities with the expenditure of transfer payments they receive. Another relevant factor is different regional growth rates in education, research and development, and related activities. Finally, the DUS growth rate is higher, the greater the earnings derived from government.

The growth sectors of the decade were the tertiary (traditionally the nonbasic or secondary sectors) and the governmental. Indeed, no DUS with more than 12.5 percent of its earnings derived from federal sources lost population in the decade, and the greater the federal contribution to local earnings, the greater the decadal growth rate. This finding is of particular importance for it emphasizes that among the unplanned consequences of the concentration of governmental expenditures in particular places are systematic impacts on the growth rates of those places. Thus, when we turn to the question of inducing growth in lagging areas, we must consider what alternative pattern might have been produced by some other pattern of regional expenditure of the federal dollar.[5]

In the context of the present study, one may add that the expenditure of the federal dollar must also be considered when the issue is one of controlling growth in rapidly-growing areas. As will be seen, this is by no means the only instance of heavy federal responsibility for the degree of local growth as well as its nature.

Population Changes

It often has been argued that urban problems could be dealt with more rationally on a metropolitan-wide basis, in contrast to the fragmentary manner characteristic of most SMSAs. The argument could be extended from the SMSA to the DUS, but for most im-

12

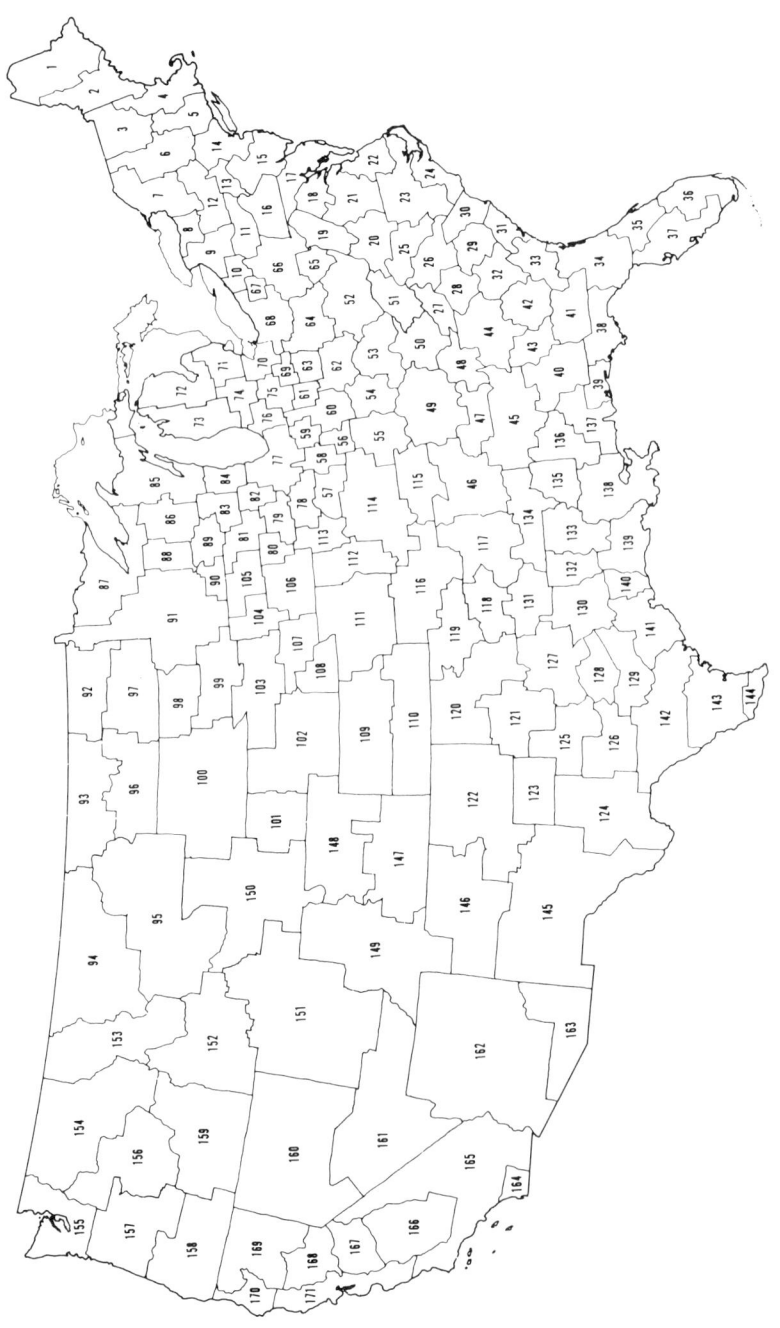

1. Bangor, Maine
2. Portland, Maine
3. Burlington, Vt.
4. Boston, Mass.
5. Hartford, Conn.
6. Albany-Schenectady-Troy, N.Y.
7. Syracuse, N.Y.
8. Rochester, N.Y.
9. Buffalo, N.Y.
10. Erie, Pa.
11. Williamsport, Pa.
12. Binghamton, N.Y.-Pa.
13. Wilkes-Barre-Hazelton, Pa.
14. New York, N.Y.
15. Philadelphia, Pa.-N.J.
16. Harrisburg, Pa.
17. Baltimore, Md.
18. Washington, D.C.-Md.-Va.
19. Staunton, Va.
20. Roanoke, Va.
21. Richmond, Va.
22. Norfolk-Portsmouth, Va.
23. Raleigh, N.C.
24. Wilmington, N.C.
25. Greensboro-Winston Salem-High Point, N.C.
26. Charlotte, N.C.
27. Asheville, N.C.
28. Greenville, S.C.
29. Columbia, S.C.
30. Florence, S.C.
31. Charleston, S.C.
32. Augusta, Ga.
33. Savannah, Ga.
34. Jacksonville, Fla.
35. Orlando, Fla.
36. Miami, Fla.
37. Tampa-St. Petersburg, Fla.
38. Tallahassee, Fla.
39. Pensacola, Fla.
40. Montgomery, Ala.
41. Albany, Ga.
42. Macon, Ga.
43. Columbia, Ga.-Ala.
44. Atlanta, Ga.
45. Birmingham, Ala.
46. Memphis, Tenn.-Ark.
47. Huntsville, Ala.
48. Chattanooga, Tenn.-Ga.
49. Nashville, Tenn.
50. Knoxville, Tenn.
51. Bristol, Va.-Tenn.
52. Huntington-Ashland, W. Va.-Ky.-Ohio
53. Lexington, Ky.
54. Louisville, Ky.-Ind.
55. Evansville, Ind.
56. Terre Haute, Ind.
57. Springfield, Ill.
58. Champaign-Urbana, Ill.
59. Lafayette-West Lafayette, Ind.
60. Indianapolis, Ind.
61. Muncie, Ind.
62. Cincinnati, Ohio-Ky.-Ind.
63. Dayton, Ohio
64. Columbus, Ohio
65. Clarksburg, W. Va.
66. Pittsburgh, Pa.
67. Youngstown-Warren, Ohio
68. Cleveland, Ohio
69. Lima, Ohio
70. Toledo, Ohio
71. Detroit, Mich.
72. Saginaw, Mich.
73. Grand Rapids, Mich.
74. Lansing, Mich.
75. Fort Wayne, Ind.
76. South Bend, Ind.
77. Chicago, Ill.
78. Peoria, Ill.
79. Davenport-Rock Island-Moline, Iowa-Ill.
80. Cedar Rapids, Iowa
81. Dubuque, Iowa
82. Rockford, Ill.
83. Madison, Wis.
84. Milwaukee, Wis.
85. Green Bay, Wis.
86. Wausau, Wis.
87. Duluth-Superior, Minn.-Wis.
88. Eau Claire, Wis.
89. La Crosse, Wis.
90. Rochester, Minn.
91. Minneapolis-St. Paul, Minn.
92. Grand Forks, N.D.
93. Minot, N.D.
94. Great Falls, Mont.
95. Billings, Mont.
96. Bismark, N.D.
97. Fargo-Moorhead, N.D.-Minn.
98. Aberdeen, S.D.
99. Sioux Falls, S.D.
100. Rapid City, S.D.
101. Scotts Bluff, Nebr.
102. Grand Island, Nebr.
103. Sioux City, Iowa-Nebr.
104. Ford Dodge, Iowa
105. Waterloo, Iowa
106. Des Moines, Iowa
107. Omaha, Nebr.-Iowa
108. Lincoln, Nebr.
109. Salina, Kans.
110. Witchita, Kans.
111. Kansas City, Mo.-Kans.
112. Columbia, Mo.
113. Quincy, Ill.
114. St. Louis, Mo.-Ill.
115. Paducah, Ky.
116. Springfield, Mo.
117. Little Rock-No. Little Rock, Ark.
118. Fort Smith, Ark.-Okla.
119. Tulsa, Okla.
120. Oklahoma City, Okla.
121. Wichita Falls, Tex.
122. Amarillo, Tex.
123. Lubbock, Tex.
124. Odessa, Tex.
125. Abilene, Tex.
126. San Angelo, Tex.
127. Dallas, Tex.
128. Waco, Tex.
129. Austin, Tex.
130. Tyler, Tex.
131. Texarkana, Tex.-Ark.
132. Shreveport, La.
133. Monroe, La.
134. Greenville, Miss.
135. Jackson, Miss.
136. Meridian, Miss.
137. Mobile, Ala.
138. New Orleans, La.
139. Lake Charles, La.
140. Beaumont-Port Arthur-Orange, Tex.
141. Houston, Tex.
142. San Antonio, Tex.
143. Corpus Christi, Tex.
144. Brownsville-Harlingen-San Bernito, Tex.
145. El Paso, Tex.
146. Albuquerque, N.M.
147. Pueblo, Colo.
148. Denver, Colo.
149. Grand Junction, Colo.
150. Cheyenne, Wyo.
151. Salt Lake City, Utah
152. Idaho Falls, Idaho
153. Butte, Mont.
154. Spokane, Wash.
155. Seattle-Everett, Wash.
156. Yakima, Wash.
157. Portland, Ore.-Wash.
158. Eugene, Ore.
159. Boise City, Idaho
160. Reno, Nev.
161. Las Vegas, Nev.
162. Phoenix, Ariz.
163. Tucson, Ariz.
164. San Diego, Calif.
165. Los Angeles-Long Beach, Calif.
166. Fresno, Calif.
167. Stockton, Calif.
168. Sacramento, Calif.
169. Redding, Calif.
170. Eureka, Calif.
171. San Francisco-Oakland, Calif.
172. Anchorage, Alaska
173. Honolulu, Hawaii

Source: Reprinted with permission from Brian J. L. Berry, *Growth Centers in the American Urban System*, vol. 1 (Cambridge, Mass.: Ballinger Publishing Company, 1973), p. 16. Copyright © 1973 Ballinger Publishing Company.

Figure 2-1. The BEA Economic Areas

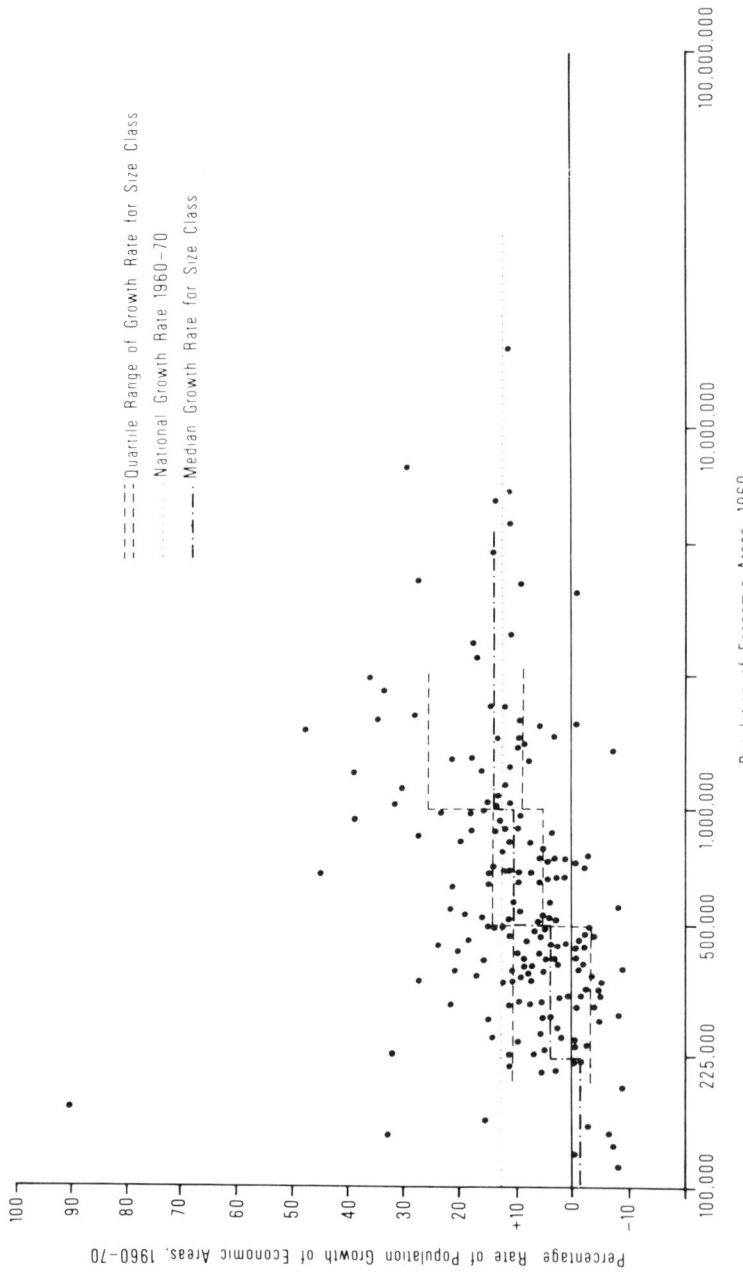

Figure 2-2. Growth Rate of the DUSs 1960-70 Related to Their Population in 1960.

Source: Reprinted with permission from Brian J. L. Berry, *Growth Centers in the American Urban System*, vol. 1 (Cambridge, Mass.: Ballinger Publishing Company, 1973), p. 22. Copyright © 1973 Ballinger Publishing Company.

mediate purposes it is difficult enough for the citizenry to maintain even the perspective of the SMSA. Where the latter is adopted, it is likely that the model being assumed is one where an influx of persons from nonmetropolitan areas is crowding the central city, forcing relatively more affluent persons (who usually happen to be white) to the suburbs. It may also be recognized that the "pull" of the suburbs may be at least as important as the "push" effect in the central city, and that, on balance, many central cities have lost population in recent years. Nevertheless, the general picture is one of continuing overall metropolitan growth. Even more sophisticated projections of future population growth assume that present trends will continue or that the nature of structural changes can be anticipated. Figure 2-3, for example, shows zones of net population in-migration between 1960 and 1970. The vast majority of communities that have expressed active concern about controlling growth obviously are found in these areas. Figure 2-4 presents one of the most frequently cited projections of the American urban landscape at the end of the century, that made by Jerome Pickard for the U.S. Commission on Population Growth and the American Future. Comparison of Figure 2-3 and Figure 2-4 makes it clear that the projected large urban regions of the future are for the most part in areas that have recently experienced relatively rapid in-migration. While many of these regions already exist, the movement to control urban growth may be viewed as an attempt to stem the increase that is expected to take place within and in proximity to existing urban areas.

However, population projections are among the more hazardous enterprises in the social sciences, and already it is apparent that present and future growth patterns will not merely continue the trends of the past several decades. For one thing, the model which assumes large flows of nonmetropolitan persons into metropolitan areas is obsolete. The rate of migration to all metropolitan areas has declined from 21 per 1,000 inhabitants per year in the first decade of the century to less than 5 per 1,000 in 1960-65. That part of total metropolitan growth accounted for by migration declined from 70 per cent to less than 30 per cent during this same period, and the present figure is down to about 20 per cent.[6]

Population increase resulting from natural increase—births over deaths—is also on the decline. The annual national rate of natural increase has dropped from 1.5 per cent in 1955 to about 0.8 per cent in 1971. Although the birth rate probably will rise somewhat as the

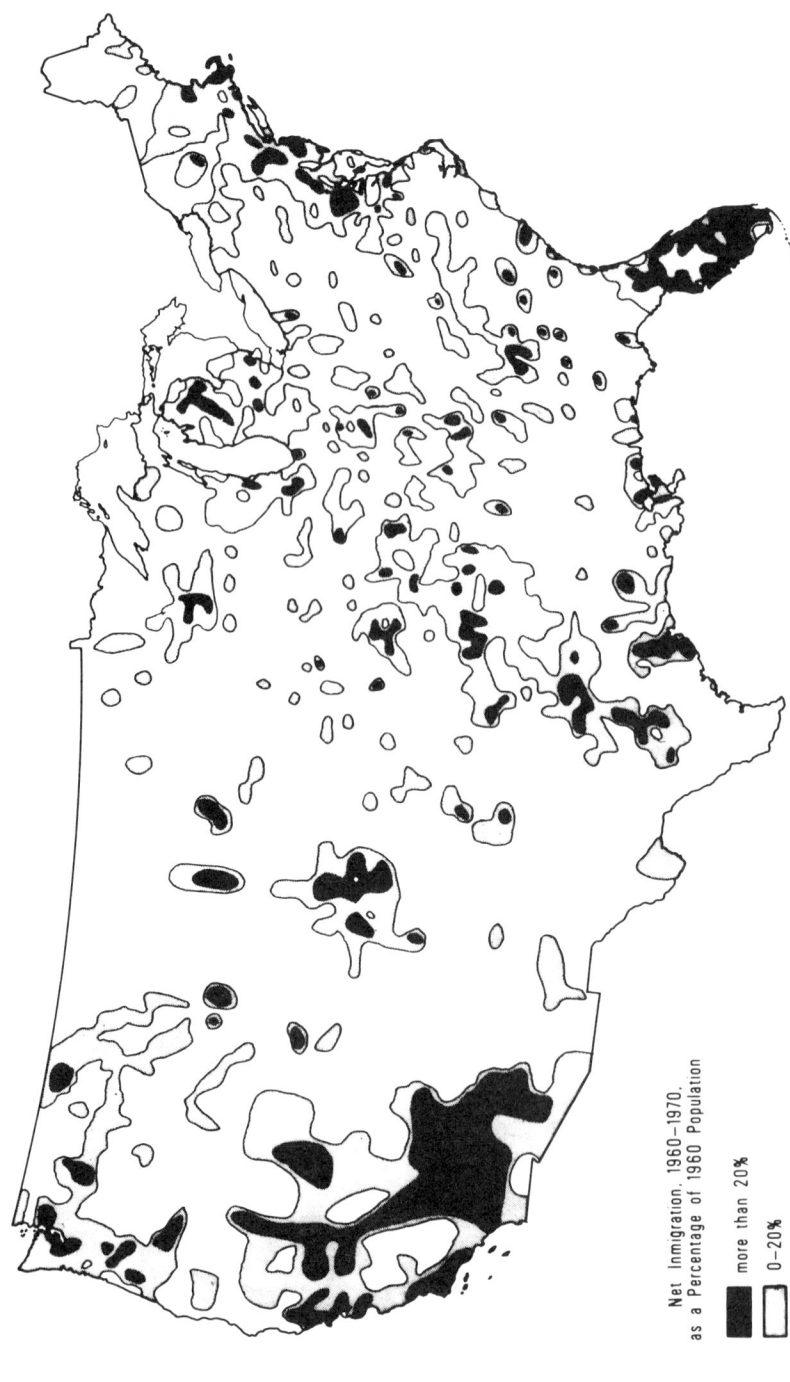

Figure 2-3. Zones of Net Immigration, 1960-70

Source: Reprinted with permission from Brian J. L. Berry, *Growth Centers in the American Urban System*, vol. 1 (Cambridge, Mass.: Ballinger Publishing Company, 1973). p. 37. Copyright © 1973 Ballinger Publishing Company.

17

Based on 2-child family projection

1. Metropolitan Belt
   1.a. Atlantic Seabord
   1.b. Lower Great Lakes
2. California Region
3. Florida Peninsula
4. Gulf Coast
5. East Central Texas—
   Red River
6. Southern Piedmont
7. North Georgia—South
   East Tennessee
8. Puget Sound
9. Twin Cities Region
10. Colorado Piedmont
11. Saint Louis
12. Metropolitan Arizona
13. Willamette Valley
14. Central Oklahoma—
    Arkansas Valley
15. Missouri—Kaw Valley
16. North Alabama
17. Blue Grass
18. Southern Coastal Plain
19. Salt Lake Valley
20. Central Illinois
21. Nashville Region
22. East Tennessee
23. Oahu Island
24. Memphis
25. El Paso—Ciudad Juarez

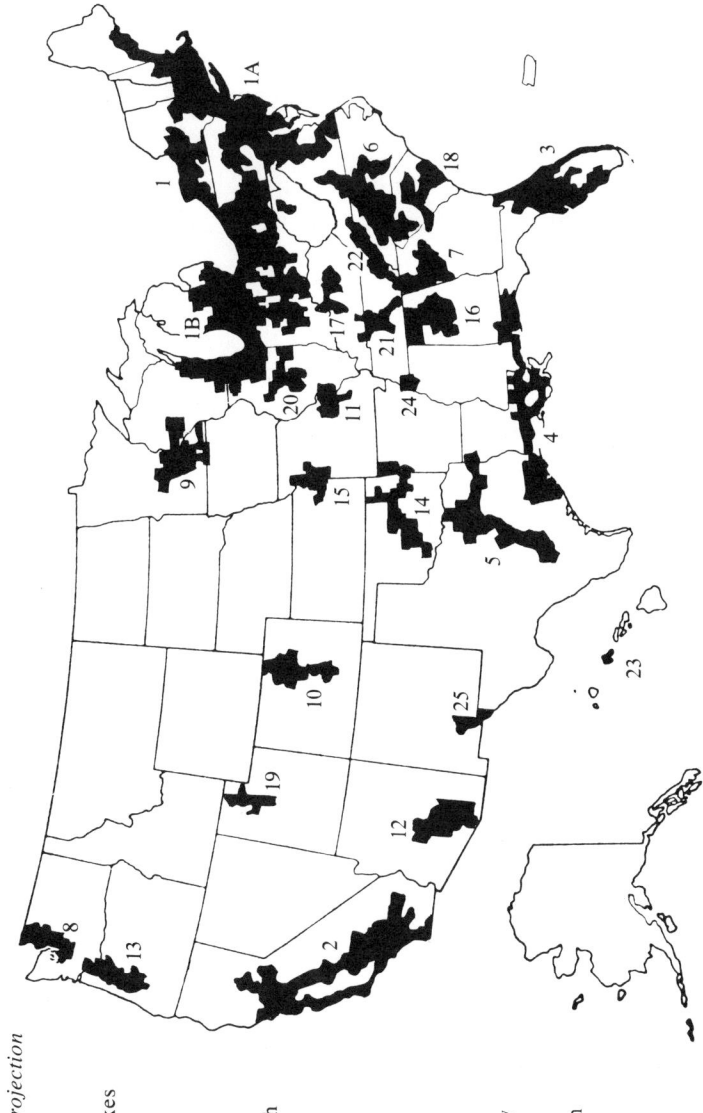

Figure 2-4. Projected Urban Regions in the Year 2000

Source: U.S. Commission on Population Growth and the American Future, *Population Distribution and Policy*, Sara Mills Mazie, ed., vol. 5 of Commission research reports (Washington, D.C.: U.S. Government Printing Office, 1972), p. 143.

persons born during the postwar "baby boom" begin to establish their own families, population growth rates that are adjusted for population composition will continue to decline.[7] At present, 44 per cent of all SMSAs lose more people than they gain through migration,[8] but in the vast majority, the deficit is more than compensated for by natural increase. A continued decline in natural increase could stabilize or even reverse growth in many SMSAs. Thus, William Alonso speculates that:

Although 91 percent of all metropolitan areas have grown in population in the last decade, it does not take much imagination to see that the drying up of migration into metropolitan areas as a whole will increase the number of net migratory losers and the extent of the net loss; this, together with the decline in the rate of natural increase, might result in some 60 to 80 metropolitan areas (*not* central cities) actually losing population by 1980, with many others achieving stationary populations. Viewed another way, national population stability will result in considerable instability among the metropolitan elements.[9]

It is frequently pointed out that military men who prepare to fight the last war over are likely to come to grief in the next one. The warning also applies to persons who make urban growth policies, in so far as any exist. No doubt, some cities that have been belatedly gearing up to cope with problems occasioned by growth might better be anticipating problems associated with stagnation or decline in population. On the other hand, some areas will continue to grow rapidly and may be able to plan so as to avoid some of the mistakes of the past. In any event, it must be recognized that he who would influence population distribution trends must first be able to influence employment opportunities. This supposes some knowledge of the economics of urban size and growth. However, before turning to this complex matter, it is appropriate to consider people's location objectives. When we speak of making spatial resource allocation more rational, it is implied that we are—in some sense—trying to increase the total level of welfare, implying in turn that we know something about the preferences that we presumably are trying to satisfy. Though this is a very shaky area, the limited evidence at hand deserves careful examination.

3 Where Do People Want to Live?

Locational Preferences

In May 1971 a major national survey concerning people's residential preferences was carried out for the Commission on Population Growth and the American Future.[1] The place of residence of the respondents is shown in Table 3-1, while preferred place of residence is shown in Table 3-2. The data in Table 3-2 indicate that over half (53 per cent) of the respondents would prefer to live in a rural or small town setting instead of a more urban environment. Another 33 per cent expressed a preference for a small urban place. In contrast, only 13 per cent preferred to live in a large urban area. This pattern is in distinct contrast to the actual distribution of the population; 32 per cent define their residence to be in a rural or small town setting, 41 per cent in a small- or medium-size city or its suburb (small urban), and 28 per cent in a large city or suburb (large urban). (See Table 3-1.)

In general, about half of the respondents preferred a location other than their current one. Moreover, those expressing a desire to live in another environment strongly preferred rural areas and smaller urban settings to large urban places. It is noteworthy that the survey results indicate that a person's current locational preference tends to be directly related to where he spent most of his childhood. People tend to have a stronger preference for the setting in which they were reared, and if they still live in this setting, the preference for staying there is even stronger—if they are white. About the same percentage of black as white respondents preferred a location other than their current one, but blacks wanted to move to more urban places. (A double sampling of blacks was used in order to ensure adequate representation and accuracy.) Clearly, blacks did not show enthusiasm for returning to the places where they were reared. For the white majority, "Whether the preference for a childhood environment is an expression of nostalgia about the past, a search for a familiar setting, or a realistic choice of one kind of living over

Table 3-1
Actual Place of Residence as Described by Respondents to Population Commission Survey, 1971

	Rural or Small Town	Small Urban	Large Urban	Number
	Per Cent			
National	32	41	28	1,708
Region				
Northeast	31	37	32	371
South	37	39	24	583
North Central	27	40	32	480
West	30	47	23	274
Age				
Under 30 years	26	47	27	468
30 years and over	35	37	28	1,219
Color				
White	34	41	25	1,362
Black	17	33	50	320
Education				
Less than high school	39	38	24	641
High school complete	29	41	29	542
Some college	22	48	30	300
College complete	21	41	39	206
Income				
Under $5,000	46	39	15	402
$5,00 to $9,999	27	45	27	487
$10,000 to $14,999	29	38	31	344
$15,000 or more	23	42	35	255

Source: Sara Mills Mazie and Steve Rawlings, "Public Attitude Towards Population Distribution Issues," U.S. Commission on Population Growth and the American Future, *Population Distribution and Policy*, Sara Mills Mazie, ed., vol. V of Commission research reports (Washington, D.C.: U.S. Government Printing Office, 1972).

another, is hard to determine. Whatever the explanation, if this preference holds true in the future, the growing generation of young people born in metropolitan areas should not have as strong a preference for small-town and rural life as do their parents, who often are of rural origin."[2]

Metropolitan Growth

In any case, nationally, over half of those questioned were in favor of federal action to slow the growth of large metropolitan areas. (See

Table 3-2
Residential Preference of Respondents to Population Commission Survey, 1971

	Rural or Small Town	Small Urban	Large Urban	No Opinion	Number
	Per Cent				
National	53	33	13	1	1,708
Residence					
Rural or small town	88	10	2	...	473
Small urban	39	55	6	...	753
Large urban	34	26	39	2	478
Region					
Northeast	58	28	14	...	371
South	57	30	12	...	583
North Central	46	37	17	...	480
West	50	38	12	...	274
Age					
Under 30 years	56	28	15	...	468
30 years and over	52	34	13	1	1,219
Color					
White	54	33	11	...	1,362
Black	33	34	33	...	320
Education					
Less than high school	57	30	12	1	641
High school complete	54	32	13	1	542
Some college	47	38	14	1	300
College complete	40	38	22	...	206
Income					
Under $5,000	57	32	10	1	402
$5,000 to $9,999	53	34	12	...	487
$10,000 to $14,999	45	29	11	...	344
$15,000 or more	45	34	21	...	255

Note: Rural or small town includes the farm, open country, or small town responses. Small urban represents small city, or medium-size city and suburb. Large urban includes the large city and its suburbs.

Source: Sara Mills Mazie and Steve Rawlings, "Public Attitude Towards Population Distribution Issues," U.S. Commission on Population Growth and the American Future, *Population Distribution and Policy*, Sara Mills Mazie, ed., vol. V of Commission research reports (Washington, D.C.: U.S. Government Printing Office, 1972).

Table 3-3). About one-third opposed such action and the remainder had no opinion. Again, there was a significant difference between blacks and whites. Fifty-four per cent of the whites were for discouraging the growth of large metropolitan areas, but only 35 per cent of the blacks took this position. "This may well be a reflection of the fact that blacks have gravitated to these places in recent years

Table 3-3
Attitudes of Respondents to Population Commission Survey Toward Whether the Federal Government Should Discourage Growth of Large Metropolitan Areas

	Should	Should Not	No Opinion	Number
	Per Cent			
National	52	33	15	1,708
Residence				
Rural or small town	51	29	20	473
Small urban	52	34	14	753
Large urban	51	36	13	478
Region				
Northeast	60	30	10	371
South	49	31	20	583
North Central	51	36	13	480
West	48	35	17	274
Age				
Under 30 years	59	29	12	468
30 years and over	49	35	16	1,219
Color				
White	54	32	14	1,362
Black	35	41	24	320
Education				
Less than high school	43	38	19	641
High school complete	57	31	12	542
Some college	61	30	9	300
College complete	64	20	16	206
Income				
Under $5,000	45	35	20	402
$5,000 to $9,999	50	36	13	487
$10,000 to $14,999	54	35	11	344
$15,000 or more	67	25	8	255

Source: Sara Mills Mazie and Steve Rawlings, "Public Attitude Towards Population Distribution Issues," U.S. Commission on Population Growth and the American Future, *Population Distribution and Policy*, Sara Mills Mazie, ed., vol. V of Commission research reports (Washington, D.C.: U.S. Government Printing Office, 1972).

in pursuit of a higher quality of life. Perhaps our large metropolitan areas have not always been the paradise they had hoped for, but blacks are nevertheless dubious about actions aimed at reversing a trend which has been one of their primary means of moving toward social and economic equality with the white population."[3]

Curiously, the size of the community in which the respondents live has little effect on the proportion favoring federal discouragement of growth in large metropolitan areas, though a somewhat higher proportion, compared with residents of other areas, of "large-urban" residents oppose such action. Support for curtailing growth is considerably higher in the Northeast than in the rest of the country. The Northeast has the highest proportion of its people living in metropolitan areas and it also has the nation's oldest cities. But it is not clear whether Northeast respondents opposing growth are actually dissatisfied with their setting or whether they find it agreeable as is but do not want future growth. Northeast respondents also had the greatest preference for a rural or small-town residence (Table 3-2), but it may be that they still wish to be in proximity to the amenities of metropolitan areas.

Proximity to Metropolitan Areas

Another study for the Population Commission provides evidence that people do, in fact, want the best of both worlds—metropolitan and nonmetropolitan. A study carried out by James Zuiches and Glenn Fuguitt in Wisconsin went beyond previous location preference surveys by adding a question concerning the desirability of proximity to a large city, defined to be over 50,000 population. As in other surveys, a high proportion (61 per cent) of the respondents expressed a desire to live in rural areas or small towns. However, only 24 per cent wanted such a place to be more than 30 miles from a central city. If the respondents' preferences were realized, 70 per cent of Wisconsin's residents would be living either in a metropolitan area or within commuting distance of it, whereas only 54 per cent at present actually live in or near such metropolitan areas. Very few metropolitan residents prefer to live beyond commuting distance, whereas somewhat over half of respondents in nonmetropolitan areas would like to live within metropolitan commuting range. Moreover, those preferring to move into metropolitan areas were younger and better educated and held higher status jobs than those who wanted to move away from metropolitan areas.

What is indicated by the Wisconsin survey is a consistency between actual and preferred location—something that was overlooked in previous surveys. "That the pattern of population change in the 1960's for Wisconsin is congruent with the preference we found can be shown by the following: Nonmetropolitan areas have grown only 3.5 percent; central cities, 5.5 percent; whereas places within the urbanized area surrounding the central cities increased 25.5 percent; and the remainder of the metropolitan areas grew 42.5 percent. A similar pattern of growth was repeated throughout the United States during 1960-1970. It seems evident that a redistribution according to personal preferences is occurring for at least some groups of the population."[4]

The extent to which one may generalize based on the Wisconsin study is debatable. For one thing, the definition of a big city as one over 50,000 population is highly conservative, even though it coincides with the minimum level required to achieve SMSA status. Also, Wisconsin is not one of the more densely-populated states and its population composition is less metropolitan than that of the nation as a whole. Thus, the value placed on proximity to large cities may be different from that in more densely populated areas, though, as indicated earlier, the evidence from the Northeast is consistent with the evidence from the Wisconsin study.

A recent national survey by the authors of the Wisconsin study[5] provides further support for the "best-of-both-worlds" hypothesis. Almost half of the respondents lived in cities with over 50,000 population, one-third within 30 miles of such a city, and 20 per cent in more distant locations. Preference patterns, however, did not appear in accord with the actual place of residence pattern. Only a quarter of the respondents would prefer to live in a large city, but one-half would like to live within commuting distance of such a place. The proportion preferring a more distant location was about the same as the proportion living there. If people actually lived where they preferred, cities over 500,000 would lose population, while rural areas near large cities would gain population.

Economists and geographers have long used graphed figures known as density gradients to describe the way population density declines as one moves away from the center of a metropolitan area toward its periphery. The density gradient for a typical nineteenth-century industrial city would look like an inverted ice cream cone. Indeed, the air traveler is still struck by the extent to which the overall skyscraper pattern of some cities still roughly resembles this configuration. But the physical appearance of the downtown buildings belies actual residential locations. As noted in the previous chapter, the most realistic economic unit of urban analysis is the DUS rather than the SMSA, even though political realities often mean that planning must be done on an SMSA basis at best. And the typical density gradient for a contemporary SMSA or DUS is much flatter than that for the nineteenth-century model. The ice cream cone has been mashed at the top and pressed out on the sides. In keeping with the location preference studies just discussed, people apparently have been, in a sense, moving toward rural amenities, yet keeping within commuting distance of urban amenities. In the national survey by Fuguitt and Zuiches, the attachment that many people felt for small towns or rural areas was apparent.

The reasons given for choosing small towns and rural areas frequently included commonly held advantages of rural life even for those preferring to live within 30 miles of a large city. This, coupled with the responses to the ranking question which showed *two-thirds of the respondents ranked big cities the least desirable* as places to live, indicates that a favorable orientation to rural and small-town life, in contrast to life in the big city, underlies the preferences of most respondents, including those wishing to live a short distance from a metropolitan center.[6]

In other words, whereas Berry (see Chapter 2) and many other urban geographers and economists emphasize that cities—and the bigger the better—are the focal points of economic and social organization, there is evidence from other sources that many people still prefer nonmetropolitan settings. The fact that these other sources usually are connected with the Department of Agriculture or else with university departments oriented toward agricultural and rural interests does not necessarily mean they are wrong. In any event, it is not our intention to become caught up here in the battle for academic suzerainty of the urban field. The most simple argument appears to be that while many people would prefer to live outside of big cities for noneconomic reasons, economic factors still exert a strong pull in the direction of metropolitan areas. For example, in the national study of Fuguitt and Zuiches, only one person in five who preferred a more rural location—even within 30 miles of a big city—did so because of better job opportunities.[7] But they also state the paradox that "if persons move to locations peripheral to large cities in order to obtain rural qualities of life, they will ultimately be thwarted in their desires, as more and more people join them."[8] As will be shown in later chapters, this may be the crux of most efforts to limit urban growth in peripheral areas; those who got there first do not want their desires thwarted.

Because we are primarily concerned here with possibilities for guiding urban growth, the relevance of residential preference survey results to proposals for promoting development in rural areas and fostering population redistribution in favor of such areas will not be pursued. In any case, there is little agreement on the matter. However, when most Americans live in metropolitan areas, but a major portion say they would prefer to live in a town or small-urban setting, some attention must be given to what people are trying to say when they voice this discontent.

Attitudes Toward Neighborhood

A recent review of attitudes toward residential location raises the point that what may be fundamentally at issue is the importance of a person's dwelling and its immediate surroundings, i.e., the neighborhood, in producing a satisfactory community life. According to this argument, people tend to prefer single-family dwellings with private yards and feel that they are more likely to obtain them in small towns.[9] However true this may be, it would seem that an even more basic issue may be that of control over the immediate environment. Thus, James Q. Wilson finds that:

It is primarily at the neighborhood level that meaningful (i.e. potentially rewarding) opportunities for the exercise of urban citizenship exist. And it is the breakdown of neighborhood controls (neighborhood self-government, if you will) that accounts for the principal concern of urban citizens. When they can neither take for granted nor influence by their actions and those of their neighbors the standards of conduct within their own neighborhood communities, they experience what to them are "urban problems"—problems that arise directly out of the unmanageable consequences of living in close proximity.

I suspect that it is this concern for the maintenance of the neighborhood community that explains in part the overwhelming preference Americans have for small cities and towns.[10]

This view, while no doubt partly correct, seems heavily influenced by the period during which it was written, the late 1960s. It was not long ago, to be sure, but we have apparently passed the time when blacks put the torch to whole neighborhoods—or at least to their own. Nevertheless, the identification of urban problems with neighborhood problems is on the right track, at least insofar as people's attitudes are concerned. The term SMSA (much less DUS!) is hardly a part of the working vocabulary of most Americans, and particularly those who live in the less desirable neighborhoods.

While this chapter has given considerable attention to *where* people want to live, it has not yet addressed the issue of *how* people perceive the quality of life in their present locales. A recent Gallup survey of over 3,000 adults, living in more than 350 places across the nation, provides unique insights in this regard. It is especially instructive to compare the proportions of people who are satisfied with the quality of life in their community (Table 3-4) and the degree of attractiveness that people attribute to their neighborhood (Table 3-5). For example, the proportion of whites who regard their neighborhood as very attractive is four times that of blacks. However, 84 per cent of whites and 44 per cent of blacks feel that their neighborhood is very attractive or fairly attractive. The corresponding values for attitude toward quality of life in the respondents' community were 78 per cent and 51 per cent. In other words, whites were more satisfied with their neighborhood than with their community, whereas blacks were more satisfied with their community than with their neighborhood. This may be a partial reflection of the fact that black neighborhoods are, in fact, usually less desirable from a physical point of view than white neighborhoods. Higher crime rates among blacks and the fact that the victims of crimes by blacks are usually other blacks may also be involved.

If attitudes toward both community quality and neighborhood attractiveness are examined in relation to size of place where respondents live, it is apparent that nonmetropolitan residents come off better in each case. Over 80 per cent of the persons living in places with under 50,000 population were satisfied with their community, compared with a corresponding national value of 75 per cent. However, only 61 per cent of the persons in places with over a million inhabitants were satisfied with their community.

Attitudes toward neighborhood attractiveness showed a distinct dichotomy between persons living in places with fewer than 50,000 persons and places larger than this value, i.e., the lower limit for an SMSA. In the 2,500 to 49,999 class, 90 per cent thought their neighborhood was very attractive or fairly attractive; the same attitudes were held by 85 per cent of the respondents from places below 2,500 population. For the larger cities, the combined very attractive and fairly attractive responses varied from 74 per cent to 76 per cent.

Table 3-4
Percentage of Americans Satisfied or Dissatisfied with the Quality of Life in Their Community, 1973

	Satisfied %	Dissatisfied %	Do Not Know %
NATIONAL	75	21	4
White	78	18	4
Nonwhite	51	44	5
One million and over	61	35	4
500,000-999,999	77	20	3
50,000-499,999	69	25	6
2,500-49,000	81	17	2
Under 2,500	84	13	3
East	73	23	4
Midwest	80	17	3
South	73	22	5
West	72	24	4

Source: The American Institute of Public Opinion (The Gallup Poll).

Table 3-5
Responses of Americans Concerning the Degree of Attractiveness of Their Neighborhood (Per Cent), 1973

	Very Attractive %	Fairly %	Unattractive %	No Answer %
NATIONWIDE	26	54	16	4
White	28	56	12	4
Nonwhite	7	37	47	9
Million and over	21	53	19	7
500,000-999,999	30	46	18	6
50,000-499,999	20	55	22	3
2,500-49,999	31	59	8	2
Under 2,500	30	55	12	3
East	26	51	17	6
Midwest	24	61	12	3
South	25	56	15	4
West	29	48	21	2

Source: The American Institute of Public Opinion (The Gallup Poll).

Broadly regional differences in attitude toward community also varied in much the same way as attitude toward neighborhood attractiveness. In each instance, the Midwest respondents were the most satisfied. Only 17 per cent of the Midwest group were dissatisfied with their community and only 12 per cent thought their neighborhood was unattractive. In contrast, the corresponding values for respondents living in the West were 24 per cent and 21 per cent.

Thus, although George Gallup sees indications "that people in this country are beginning to think in terms of the region as a whole rather than in terms of their immediate surroundings,"[11] his own data still reveal a close association between perception of neighborhood attractiveness and perception of community quality. Still, many people would like to see better community planning. Gallup reports that:

All persons in a survey conducted in August [1973] were asked to rate the job being done by their local governments in planning for the future growth of housing in their communities.

The national findings show a majority of 55 per cent saying their local governments have done "only a fair" or a "poor" job, compared to 29 per cent who say an "excellent" or a "good" job.

Remarkably little difference is noted by region of the nation or in terms of city or community size.

Only about one person in six does not express an opinion on the job being done by their local elected officials on planning. It should be borne in mind, of course, that some survey respondents may be basing their opinions on present visible aspects of local planning rather than on knowledge of specific steps being taken or contemplated by local planning boards.

Nevertheless, the findings clearly indicate that many Americans feel that their local governments are not on top of the situation.

Their specific complaints range from the belief that planning boards spend too much of their time reacting to present problems instead of trying to anticipate future problems, that planners are too frequently lacking in imagination, or are motivated only by self-interest.[12]

On the other hand, a Gallup Poll found that six persons out of ten would be willing to serve on committees dealing with local problems, if they were asked to serve.[13] "The Question is," concludes Gallup, "can plans be developed to take advantage of the typical citizen's willingness to participate in the betterment of America?"[14] And, one may add, how informed will such plans be? The chapters that follow attempt to bring to bear on this issue the state of the art of the economics of urban size and form.

4 Some Limitations of Economic Base and Other Models of Urban Growth

Analyzing Urban Growth

The dissatisfaction that many have registered concerning the quality of life in big cities has been accompanied by a profusion of movements throughout the country to check or retard further urban growth. For example, the Austin SMSA, a pleasant university and state government center located in the central Texas hill and lake country, grew by nearly 40 per cent during the 1960s. Bureau of the Census estimates indicate that the area grew by another 7.7 per cent between 1970 and 1972, not counting the recent addition of a neighboring county to the SMSA. A local newspaper editorial complains that: "If there has been a single phenomenon that most accurately portrays Austin in the past decade it has been the city's incredible rate of growth and the corollaries of that growth. The subdivisions multiplying like jackrabbits, the massive apartment complexes gouged out of quiet, peaceful neighborhoods, the . . . . freeways decking and double-decking their way through the city: all these are inevitables in a city with a growth rate like Austin's."[1] Although a survey made in 1972 showed that 80 per cent of Austin's people would like to see growth stopped at the 350,000 level—a figure which the present population is rapidly approaching—the mayor sees no possibility of slowing or stopping growth, and the Chamber of Commerce actively continues to recruit new firms. The local newspaper editorial just cited goes on to remark that: "The Chamber's activities can be easily explained by the Smithian dictums of capitalist self-interest. For some reason, though, the Chamber goes to strange lengths to justify their activity. Vic Mathias, the Chamber's executive vice-president, says the motivating factor behind the [recruitment of industry] fund is an effort to 'ensure that job opportunities can keep pace with Austin's growth.' Now, we fear Mr. Mathias puts the cart before the horse."

This indeed would appear to be the case. Those who would control growth must first be in a position to control employment opportunities. In addition, they must have some understanding of the mechanisms by which they expand. Economists have come up with various theories to explain why and how cities grow, but many of the discipline's traditional tools have come under increasing criticism in this regard. In a survey of regional-planning policies, Benjamin Higgins notes that "the branch of economic theory underlying regional planning (location theory) is in a particularly unsatisfactory state, providing only limited guidance for policy formation."[2] Eric Lampard similarly finds that, on operational grounds,

> the general theory of location and space economy is found wanting. . . . The theory is intended to determine locations in a framework of general equilibrium; it requires optimal behavior by producers and consumers throughout the system. But quite apart from the problem of handling so many complex interrelations, the outcome is still a static system that is not geared to the analysis of locational transformation. . . . The dependence of the general theory on what, in the last analysis is virtually a single-factor explanation, namely the systematically variable cost of surmounting distance under *ceteris paribus* conditions, renders its particular solutions of little more than formal interest to the student of historical development.[3]

E.A.G. Robinson, writing on location theory and regional economics, finds that as one attempts to relax the assumptions of Lösch and Weber, the results "become more and more unreal and inconsistent with one's analysis."[4] And Lloyd Rodwin argues that the limitations of location theory are best illustrated in the writings of Walter Isard, the most distinguished scholar in this field:

> In his major work on location theory [*Location and Space Economy*] he touches on the problem of determining "the optimal spatial distribution and hierarchy of cities of different size," and he specifically poses the question: "Given a network of cities and corresponding patterns of land use, along what channels should changes in the structure of this network and these patterns be fostered in order to attain a situation closer to optimum?" But, after a brief discussion of the agglomeration aspects of location theory, he concludes that there is "little to say beyond the obvious; units are attracted to or repelled from cities according to a simple comparison of advantages and disadvantages generated by these cities."[5]

Similarly, many economists have contented themselves with analyzing urban growth within the framework of neoclassical regional growth theory. However, this approach has proven to be irrelevant to issues of prime concern in regional policy.

Features of the real world that are not easily admitted, if at all, into the neoclassical world such as increasing returns, oligopolistic competition and uncertainty figure prominently in any analysis of the space economy. Had the spatial dimension been introduced into aggregate growth analysis at an early stage in its development, neoclassical models would not have had such a long survival capacity. Many people would now accept that neoclassical growth theory is now dead (though there are still many others trying to revive the corpse), but the deathbed scene has been rather prolonged. One reason for this is that much of the literature has consisted of elegant nit-picking. We can note Sen's comments on this point: "the extent of controversy may not be a good guide to the innate importance of an issue" and "the selection of topics for work in growth economics is guided much more by logical curiosity than by a taste for relevance." The working assumptions and abstractions that the neoclassicist uses as a starting point for his analysis could never be justified in a world which recognizes the existence of space as well as time. Space is incompatible with perfect competition, complete certainty, marginal adjustments in prices, outputs and locations, and the other background conditions of the neoclassical world. In other words, although a weak case for neoclassical models can be made in aggregate growth theory there is no case at all in regional analysis.[6]

If classical-location theory and neoclassical-growth theory have little to tell the decision-maker concerned with urban policy, there is one explanation for urban and regional growth that has been given considerable attention by planners—or at least by their well-paid consultants. This is economic-base (or export-base) analysis. Because of its relative ubiquity it needs to be critically examined at some length.

Economic-Base Analysis

The economic-base approach emphasizes the importance of events outside a given area in determining the area's levels of income, employment, and output. Two economic sectors are identified: the *basic* sector, which sells to markets located outside the given area; and the *service* sector, which sells to markets within the given area. The major premise of the analysis is that exports play the most important role in the economic growth and well-being of a region, because basic employment generates income for local residents that is spent on goods and services that in turn generate service employment. The ratio between basic and service activities, usually measured in terms of employment or income, represents a multiplier.

Thus, if basic employment is 10,000 and service employment 20,000, any change in basic employment will result (though not instantaneously) in a readjustment so that the 1:2 ratio is maintained. For example, if basic employment doubles to 20,000, service employment will double in response to 40,000.

An economic-base study involves many practical problems. Along with normal difficulties in obtaining reliable data there are questions of the proper delineation of the area, the most relevant unit of measurement, and the classification of industries into their proper sectors.[7]

Employment is normally used as the unit of measurement because of relative ease of obtaining data. However, the same employment increases in industries paying different wage levels will result in different secondary effects. Employment data also fail to reflect transfer payments and incomes to factors of production other than labor. Correcting for part-time and seasonal employment presents another problem. Using payroll data would do away with the problem of interindustry wage differentials but would still not make allowance for nonlabor factors of production. Also, heavy concentration of salaries toward the upper end of the scale in an industry could mean a higher rate of saving and less expenditure in proportion to money earned than in other industries. Another alternative would be to use value-added data computed from sales figures, but the practical difficulties and cost of this approach are often prohibitive.

Segregation of basic and service activities would be simple if all industries were purely one or the other, but this is rarely the case. The best method for identifying basic and service components is the direct method of a market survey. By questionnaire and interview, the location of each firm's market can be determined and the basic-service ratio thereby determined. For example, assuming employment is the unit of measure, if 60 per cent of a firm's sales are to customers outside the area and 40 per cent to local customers, then 60 per cent of the firm's employment would be allocated to the basic sector and 40 per cent to the service sector. This method allows for the proper designation of linked activities if the final destination of the product can be determined. Obviously, there are disadvantages to this direct method such as its cost, the length of time required to complete the survey, and the possibility that the estimates or the sales records will be inaccurate with respect to the destination of the sales. However, indirect methods are plagued with far more limitations.

Perhaps the most widely used indirect measure of "export" employment is the location quotient. This method is based on the assumption that the special characteristics of the area economy are shown by the extent to which it differs from the nation as a whole. The formula used is:

$$\frac{\text{Local employment in a given industry}}{\text{Total local employment}} \div \frac{\text{National employment in the same industry}}{\text{Total national employment}}$$

The degree to which the location quotient exceeds unity determines the degree of export employment assigned to any given industry. But this assumes that consumption patterns, production functions, and the industry mix in the area concerned are all similar to the national average, which is not likely.

Another simple indirect method that merits only passing attention is the minimum requirement technique. This method involves taking several areas similar to the one under study and calculating for each industry in these areas the percentage of the area labor force that industry employs. Then, for each industry, the percentages from all areas are ranked and the lowest percentage is considered that necessary to serve an area's needs. All employment in other areas above this amount is considered export employment. The obvious difficulty here is that the method is so arbitrary. How can one be sure that the smallest percentage is not an unusual case? Or, if to guard against such unusual cases, a new criterion is established such as counting up a certain number from the bottom, then where does one make the cutoff?

There is little doubt as to the preferability of the direct market survey over the indirect methods in the determination of the basic sector. However, the indirect methods, particularly the location quotient, continue to be widely used because of their simplicity and ease of handling.

As a descriptive device the export-base theory can provide insights into the sources of income and employment in the area under study. But major problems arise when it is used as a tool for prediction. Even short-run projections of employment or income derived from applying the base-service ratio may be plagued by the fact that nonequilibrium conditions may exist, whereas the basic-service ratio assumes that the two sectors are in equilibrium with respect to each other. For example, in both the upswing and downswing of national business cycles, the sectors will be in disequilibrium. Local-service sectors tend to lag on both the upswing and downswing in export activity, thereby causing the ratio to be lower during periods of export expansion and higher during periods of contraction than would be the case in equilibrium.[8]

Also some types of bases are much more volatile cyclically than others, and, thus, qualitative changes in the base may occur. The common example is the durable goods industries, which register large fluctuations, as compared with the consumption goods industries. Therefore, the degree to which a base is specialized in particular industries will determine the nature of the reaction of the ratio during national business cycles. Of course, there are regional economic cycles as well. If the regional economy is experiencing a limited recession while the national economy is not, certain productive factors may be stimulated to move from the region. Also, areas that are greatly dependent on seasonal activities as their source of basic income may have their ratio drastically affected by a sudden curtailment of those activities due to bad weather, strikes, or other circumstances. The inference to be drawn is that an incorrect ratio would be applied when the ratio was calculated during one of these periods of disequilibrium.

The size of the multiplier also depends a great deal upon the availability of idle and inefficiently used resources. If resources are fully employed, an increase in exports will lead to a matching decrease in the production of other goods and no change in overall activity, and the multiplier will be zero.[9] There is another situation in which service employment might be expected to remain stationary while basic employment is changing. If there was a tendency for the employees added to the basic sector to save heavily or spend outside the community, then service employment would not be likely to respond positively.[10]

Another problem arises when a decline in exports is expected. By the assumptions of economic-base theory, one would expect a proportional decrease in the service sector. However, it is not reasonable to expect activities that form the nucleus of the service sector to depart promptly from the scene. These enterprises would not immediately be affected to any great degree and would show signs of decline only when labor out-migration began to occur.

The size of the multiplier is also dependent upon the particular export activity that undergoes change and, therefore, the "average" value used is not necessarily applicable to any specific export activity. The increase in exports gives rise to new import requirements by the exporting industry. But suppose Industry A imports a large portion of its intermediate import requirements, whereas Industry B purchases most of its intermediate imports locally. The appropriate multiplier to apply to an increase in exports of Industry B would be much larger than that to be applied to Industry A. The exact size of the multiplier in any case would depend upon such factors as the marginal (extra) propensity to save, the marginal propensity to consume domestic goods, and the extent of each industry's linkages with other industries in the region. Therefore, different exports are likely to have different effects on income and employment of a particular region, making the fixed multiplier applied to all export changes quite inappropriate.

In spite of the short-run difficulties, the harshest criticisms of export-base analysis have been directed at its limitations—some of which have been anticipated—with respect to long-run forecasting. Changes in markets, raw material sources, and transport rates can make an urban area either more or less specialized in various activities. Regional and national shifts in tastes and purchasing power will have a varying range of spatial influence on basic activities. And perhaps most important, technological advance and consequent productivity changes may greatly alter the nature of an area's economic base.

While attempts may be made to anticipate long-run changes and make appropriate adjustments in the base-service ratio, the fact is that the export-base model has been shown to be a poor predictor of urban growth.[11] The essential reason is that it simply is not able to come to grips with the dynamics of change. Indeed, not only export-base analysis, but also location theory, central-place theory, input-output analysis, urban hierarchy studies, shift-share analysis, industrial-complex analysis, and gravity models, have often proven inadequate for policy purposes because they have failed to take into account the changing nature of the actual determinants of the location of economic activity.[12] (Adequate discussion of these approaches is beyond the scope of this volume; the interested reader should consult several of the large and growing number of urban and regional economic textbooks.)

The emphasis given in classical-location theory to minimizing transportation costs, for example, may be contrasted to the decline in importance of shipping costs of heavy and cumbersome goods. Long-distance transfer costs have been significantly reduced, while the rapid movement of relatively light but highly elaborated products has increased in importance, as has the need to communicate information and intangible services. Moreover, whereas industrial location in the past was heavily influenced by factors such as energy sources, water, and transportation facilities, entrepreneurs today tend to be more attracted by "external economies of agglomeration" of the kind that will be discussed shortly. Economic activity also has become increasingly footloose. It has been estimated that today only about 7 per cent of the labor force needs to be located close to natural resources, whereas only several decades ago 30 per cent were resource-bound. The trend is for the labor force to be potentially footloose and to locate in proximity to consumers, who themselves are relatively footloose. Economic opportunity, therefore, is increasingly associated with capital and human skill and not with land and natural resources.[13]

Tertiary Activities

Among tertiary activities, the increasingly prominent place of amenities must be noted. The footloose nature of many activities is counterbalanced by noneconomic factors that enter into the choice of location of people and firms. Rising standards of living, more leisure, greater mobility, and better education make the quality of life a crucial factor in many location decisions. The quality of life offered by a locale is geared to the quality of its educational institutions, its climate, and its cultural and recreational opportunities, and except for climate, these are variables whose enhancement is "the result of community action and a will to attain high standards in the design of urban culture."[14]

Finally, a number of studies of the relative importance of various plant-location factors from the viewpoint of industry have indicated the importance of markets.[15] This does not deny the importance of tertiary activities because market and tertiary factors are mutually reinforcing. Because they deal with such functions as communications, construction, trade, finance, government, the professions, and recreation, tertiary activities are, by and large, closely tied to markets.[16]

Viewed in these terms, long-run urban growth is more a function of the service sector—in the broadest possible sense—than of the so-called basic activities. Even on the economist's own terms, the architects and city planners who have identified the essence of the metropolis with skyscrapers appear to have been more correct than the economists who have had their eyes fixed on the grimy factories. A competitive service sector is necessary to replace stagnating basic activities with vigorous new ones.[17] Wilbur Thompson puts the matter in the following terms:

> The economic base of the larger metropolitan area is, then, the creativity of its universities and research parks, the sophistication of its engineering firms and financial institutions, the persuasiveness of its public relations and advertising agencies, the flexibility of its transportation networks and utility systems, and all the other dimensions of infrastructure that facilitate the quick and orderly transfer from old dying bases to new growing ones. A diversified set of current exports—"breadth"—softens the shock of exogenous change, while a rich infrastructure—"depth"—facilitates the adjustment to change by providing the socioeconomic institutions and physical facilities needed to initiate new enterprises, transfer capital from old to new forms, and retrain labor.[18]

What contemporary economics brings to urban policy decision-makers is, therefore, not simply a collection of intellectual games played out by a handful of professors with a vested interest in the continuation of the games, but also genuine attempts to understand—even if only in a rough-hewn way for the time being—the forces that are shaping the evolution of our cities. This is not to say that the export-base model and other approaches criticized in this chapter are wholly without merit. Nevertheless, their relevance to decision-makers, even if not developed here, remains for now rather limited.

Key Concepts

Key concepts in the body of economic thought that admits to attempting to deal directly with relevant policy issues are themselves rather vague. These are *agglomeration economics* and *innovation*. Economists, including myself, are disposed toward conceptual frameworks that are amenable to quantification. Unfortunately, it is difficult to obtain measured observations of agglomeration economies and innovations. Perhaps they are akin to golden ages —no one knew they were there until they had passed. In any case, these concepts do underlie many fruitful efforts to develop an economics of urban growth and size. And the negative counterparts of agglomeration economies, the diseconomies, play an essential role in arguments concerning whether or not cities are too big. Emphasis will now shift to the positive contributions of urban economics to the understanding of urban growth.

5 Advantages of the City

External Economies

Externalities have been defined as "the impacts of the activities of households, public agencies, or enterprises which are exerted otherwise than through the market. They are, in other words, relationships other than those between buyer and seller."[1] Originally the term *external economies* was used to denote the cost reductions experienced by individual firms in a growing industry. The relevant economies (service facilities, specialized education, etc.) were external to the firm but internal to the industry. More recently the term has been used to describe any economies of operation that are external to the firm but result from the previous presence of other firms (whether in the same industry or not) and social infrastructure such as roads, schools, and utilities. External economies are, therefore, external to the firm but internal to the city or region.

From the perspective of the economist "a city is a dynamic system of interrelated and interdependent markets characterized by great density and specialization of economic actors as well as certain institutional conditions that influence decision making by many different governments, each of which has limited authority and competence. These markets serve and are served by large numbers of persons and firms located in relatively close proximity."[2] It is the great proximity in cities that generates so many externalities. As Werner Hirsch puts it, "The city is where externalities abound; and it is the prevalence of these externalities that make a city what it is."[3]

Harry Richardson has made a useful distinction among business, household, and social external economies of agglomeration.[4] Business-agglomeration economies include access to specialized business services; sources of capital; labor-market economies in the form of more varied skills, greater elasticity of labor supplies, superior training, and better-organized worker-placement services; a larger stock of managerial and professional talent; good public services; cultural amenities; opportunities for specialization because of the large market (product specialization, technical externalities, transport cost savings); economies of information and communication, especially where face-to-face contact is involved; greater adaptability and flexibility in the use of fixed capital; and last, but probably not least, the presence of a variety of business-entertainment facilities (whose existence, it may be added, often depends on the liberal tax deductions allowed for business-entertainment expenses).

Household-agglomeration economies would include opportunities for earning higher incomes, and a wide variety of jobs, shopping facilities, public services, leisure and cultural amenities, and housing. The efficient provision of major educational facilities, public transportation, hospitals, entertainment facilities, and other types of social infrastructure usually requires some minimum population-size threshold, though there may be a levelling off in many benefits in the medium size range.

Then there are the more nebulous social-agglomeration economies. This refers to the functions performed by cities as centers of innovation, and the role of cities in transmitting innovation through the urban hierarchy and to urban hinterlands.

Innovations

Wilbur Thompson has suggested that, "The large urban area would seem to have a great advantage in the critical functions of invention, innovation, promotion, and rationalization of the new. The stabilization and even institutionalization of entrepreneurship may be the principal strength of the large urban area."[5] Thompson's argument is based in part on the notion that a large population ensures a steady flow of talented people native to the area. A city of 50,000 may give birth to one commercial or industrial genius per decade but may be caught between geniuses, as it were, in the event of some economic tribulation such as the closing of a major plant. In contrast, a metropolitan area of 5 million would have an average flow of 10 such geniuses per year, so that a serious prolonged crisis in local economic leadership would be very unlikely. It may be noted that Thompson is talking only about locally-born leadership. However, if household-agglomeration economies are taken into account it is certain that net-migration flows will increase further the number of geniuses in the large city relative to other areas.

But the issue is by no means solely one of the spatial distribution of geniuses. Even more important is the institutionalization of many entrepreneurial functions. The degree to which services, in the broadest sense, have become the real economic base of larger cities was emphasized at the end of the preceding chapter. "As we become more of a service-oriented economy, the city itself becomes the very product that is being redesigned and re-engineered—becomes the experiment as well as the laboratory. Small wonder that the largest metropolitan areas can be so little concerned with promoting area industrial development, compared with the frantic activities of this kind conducted by the smaller areas."[6] The concentration of innovation in larger cities has been extended by Thompson into a more general theory of how industry that is born in large cities trickles down from them to smaller cities in the urban hierarchy.

Industries filter down through the system of cities, from places of greater to lesser industrial sophistication. Most often, the highest skills are needed in the difficult, early stage of mastering a new process, and skill requirements decline steadily as the production process is rationalized and routinized with experience. As the industry slides down the learning curve, the high wage rates of the more industrially sophisticated innovating areas become superfluous. The aging industry seeks out industrial backwaters where the cheaper labor is now up to the lesser demands of the simplified process.[7]

And it is, of course, small towns and rural areas that constitute the lowest rung of the filtering process. Thus, Thompson argues that a filter-down theory of industrial location goes far in explaining why the

smaller, less industrially advanced area struggles to achieve an average rate of growth out of enlarging shares of slow-growth industries, which were attracted by the area's low wages. It would seem that both the larger industrial centers from which, and the smaller areas to which, industries filter down must run to stand still (at the national average growth rate); the larger areas do, however, run for higher stakes.

The economic development of the smaller, less developed urban area would seem to require that it receive each successive industry a little earlier in its life cycle, to acquire the industry at a point in time when it still has both substantial job-forming potential and high-skill work. Only by upgrading the labor force on the job and by generating the higher incomes (fiscal capacity) needed to finance better schools can the area hope to break out of its underdevelopment trap.[8]

Thompson thus maintains that in the process of industrial filtering in the national system of cities, invention, or at least innovation, takes place more than proportionally in the larger metropolitan areas of industrially mature regions. However, as industries age and their technology matures, skill requirements fall and competition forces them to relocate to lower wage areas. The lower an urban area in the skill and wage hierarchy, the older an industry tends to be when it arrives, and the slower its national growth rate. Intermediate-level places tend to fashion a growth rate somewhat above the national average out of growing shares of slow-growing industries, but in smaller places the positive change in share weakens and erodes to zero, leading to slower than average growth and net out-migration, or even to absolute employment and population decline in the smallest places.

In Chapter 2 it was shown that Brian Berry's analysis of economic change within the national urban system tended to confirm Thompson's theory. My own studies of the spatial decentralization of industry to nonmetropolitan areas that have recently grown after previous stagnation or decline in population also lends support to this position.[9] Nevertheless, it should be emphasized that we are talking here essentially about manufacturing decentralization and not about the decentralization of tertiary activities; even though the latter may be decentralizing within metropolitan areas or shifting among metropolitan areas, there is relatively little movement to nonmetropolitan areas.

When discussing tertiary activities there may be a tendency to neglect the fact that the advantages of larger cities as centers of innovation are closely bound up with the production of information and communications. Information exchange for its own sake among specialists, for example scientists, eventually raises the level of sophistication and technology in urban areas, and in consequence, per-capita income also will increase. A second kind of information exchange involves financial transactions between buyers and sellers who hope to benefit from it. Advertisements, sales personnel, brokers, inventories, catalogs, market research, phone calls, and similar costs are incurred in order to facilitate the diffusion of knowledge about potential demanders and suppliers and their goods and services, as well as about the prices that can be expected to prevail.

Thus it appears that highly advanced postindustrialized urban economies are favored by extremely large amounts of pertinent information which, produced and exchanged at low cost, can greatly enhance the economy's efficiency. Under these conditions firms can make even fuller use of their entrepreneurial capacities, inventiveness, availability of capital, and access to new technology. Also, their knowledge of and access to resources, including labor, is improved, together with their understanding of today's and tomorrow's markets. Competition has been sharpened and so has the demand for product production, distribution, and market innovation.[10]

In addition, it has been argued that no matter where a growth-inducing innovation takes place in the nation's system of cities, it is likely to appear soon in some or all of the largest cities. The latter would tend to adopt the innovation because of their "high contact probabilities" with many other places. Small places would tend to adopt late, if at all, because they have relatively few nonlocal goods and services transactions.[11]

It may be noted that while some writers emphasize the role of communications in promoting the growth of large cities, others point out that in the electronic age it is no longer necessary to cluster together in close proximity. In this view, most of the functions performed in downtown offices could just as well be done from homes; or if this is not yet the case, it could be if telecommunications technology were really turned loose. Moreover, many of the consumption amenities that were formerly only available in big cities are now available in the home. In cities where professional football games are being played, many times more people watch the action in their living rooms than from the stands; even many ticket holders prefer to view the games at home. Pianist Glenn Gould maintains that the concert hall is a dead letter in the future; his performances are now limited to recordings. Of course, there will always be people who want to experience cultural and entertainment activities directly, and for them, only cities beyond a fairly large threshold size will do. Also, many people simply do not want to stay home all the time. Preservation of the life-style associated with the tight-knit nuclear family does not have the attraction it once did. In any case, even though it is not difficult to see that innovations now originate in large cities or are rapidly picked up by them, one can readily envisage alternative work and residence patterns made possible by new communications technology. And these patterns may be just as productive, for the appropriate tertiary activities, as those now prevailing, and even more satisfying from the perspective of the household.

Income and City Size

If agglomeration economies and innovations are the main propulsive mechanisms in the urban growth process, it should also be recognized that there is considerable evidence indicating that per capita income increases with city size, i.e., effective demand (purchasing power) present in the city grows at a faster rate than population. William Alonso reports that in every country for which he had data on local product per capita (or some index of it such as income or wages), it rose with urban size.[12] The best figures available were those for the German Federal Republic and Japan. In the former, gross community product per capita (1964) increased by 40 per cent from the smaller cities (20,000 to 50,000) to those above 500,000. The Japanese data were organized by density and by prefecture, with the densest areas corresponding to the largest cities. Mean per-capita income (thousands of yen per capita in 1965) steadily increased from 188 in prefectures with a density less than 200 persons per square kilometer, to 340 where the corresponding density value was over 3,000. Turning to American data,

Many studies over the years have established that in the United States, for data grouped by city size, there is a strong and steady rise in income, of about 30 per cent depending on the size of classes and income definition used. In keeping with sociologists who have looked into various correlates of urban size, Schnore has concluded that, "Of all the differences among communities of different size revealed in this study, perhaps the most striking is the pronounced direct relationship between size of place and income." However, since group data tends to subsume intra-class variance, I have experimented with regressions of income on population. In a simple logarithmic regression . . . metropolitan population accounted for 42 per cent of the variance in mean per capita incomes. This is indeed remarkable if one considers the great diversity among cities of climate, resource endowment and history. The relation is only slightly diminished when metropolitan incomes are deflated by local cost of living in the smaller set of metropolitan areas for which the information is available.[13]

In the popular imagination, big cities are associated with a high incidence of poverty, probably because the poor are concentrated there in large absolute numbers. In fact, though, the proportion of the population in poverty is two and a half times greater in nonmetropolitan than in metropolitan areas, and comparisons among cities show that the incidence of poverty declines sharply as city size increases.[14]

Emphasis was given in the last chapter to people's apparent desire to reside where they can enjoy the best of both metropolitan and nonmetropolitan amenities. In fact, proximity to opportunities in other cities, like size of city in which a person resides, is directly associated with per capita income. In a test of this relationship Alonso examined the influence of both absolute population size and the constellation of urban opportunities available to a person or a firm at a given location on mean per capita income (1959) in metropolitan areas.[15] Considering that the analysis disregarded local resources, social, economic and political history, locational advantages, climate, and numerous other relevant variables, it was remarkable that these two variables alone accounted for better than one-fourth of the variance in per-capita incomes. The conclusion to be drawn is that: "It is misleading to consider only size, which is a measure of immediate opportunities, while neglecting the broader context of opportunities in other cities. Big and small must be qualified in their setting; whereas it may be quite good to be smaller in a dense setting, it may be necessary to be quite big in an isolated one. Policies of small and far, which are not uncommon, perhaps should be small and near, and big and far."[16]

The higher per-capita income levels associated with larger-city size, or more generally, with greater proximity to opportunities within the framework of the national system of cities, are also associated with the attainment of numerous other goal variables. A study of sixty variables representing the full set of goals actually sought by metropolitan areas indicated that income indicators are the best single measures of overall goal attainment. If one were limited to specifying only a small number of goal dimensions, the goals that could not be subsumed under income would primarily be physical goals, e.g., purity of air and open space. Thus, economic growth and physical planning are complementary aspects of efforts to attain generally accepted objectives associated with urban living.[17] Moreover, Alonso is not alone in suggesting that "even the largest cities have not yet reached excessive sizes from the point of view of growth and productivity."[18] But can it be said that bigger is always better? Or at least better in terms of the immediately foreseeable future?

Optimum Size

Few economists would give a dogmatic response to these questions because to do so would require knowing more than we do about the nature of optimum-city sizes, which would vary not only with a city's place in the national urban system, but also with how a given population is distributed within a city, i.e., on the particular form of urbanization. The notion of an optimum size also would depend on what variable or set of variables was chosen to be optimized; and even if the variables could be quantified—which they usually cannot be—their selection obviously would be highly subjective. Nevertheless, some worthwhile general things are known about the disadvantages of large size, and the issue of comparing the advantages and disadvantages of various city sizes can be discussed intelligently even if all the relevant variables cannot be measured, and even if there may be disagreement on the weights to be attached to relevant variables.

6 When is a Big City too Big?

In the previous chapter stress was given to the advantages resulting from the proximity of people and economic activities in cities. However, the external economies that attract people and firms to cities are accompanied by their negative counterpart, external diseconomies, that are reflected in traffic congestion, air, water and noise pollution, social disorder, physical blight, high public investment requirements, and similar phenomena.

The larger places have a clear and sizable advantage in such areas as cheaper and more flexible transportation and utility systems, better research and development facilities, a more skilled and varied labor supply, and better facilities for educating and retraining workers. Further, these economies of scale are captured by private business as lower private costs; at the same time private business is able to slough off on society various social costs that its presence imposes, such as its addition to traffic congestion and air pollution. If, then, the external diseconomies of business-created noise, dirt, congestion, and pollution are some increasing function of city size and/or density, factor market prices are biased in favor of large urban areas, and understate the true market costs of production in the metropolis. In the absence of sophisticated public policy and the even more sophisticated public management that would be needed to implement price reform, factor markets so biased promote urban growth and great size.[1]

High Population Density

While many urban problems may be related more to high population density than to large population size as such, there is a direct association between the two. The data in Table 6-1 show that the proportion of people who feel they live under congested conditions increases consistently with size of place in which they live. Only 3 per cent of the population in rural areas feels that their residence is congested, and only 10 per cent of the population in small towns feels similarly. However, the proportion jumps to 20 per cent in the smaller metropolitan areas and to over one-fourth of the total in places over 500,000 population. The proportion of blacks who feel that they live in congested conditions is particularly noteworthy; it is two and a half times greater than the national proportion.

Many persons have maintained that sheer density has undesirable social effects. For example, René Dubos believes that crowded environments may promote an excessive secretion of various hormones, with a number of possibly harmful consequences ranging from social aberrations and cannibalism to complete social unresponsiveness. He further believes that mob hysteria and juvenile delinquency may also be linked to crowding.[2] A study of the backgrounds of 1,660 residents of a middle-class neighborhood in New York City showed that stress and mental disorder were directly related; in a report on these findings to the American Psychological Association, Dr. Thomas Langner summarized the situation as "the more the unmerrier."[3] Similarly, Dr. John Christian of Philadelphia's Albert Einstein Medical Center has reported that overcrowding may lead to mass psychosis and psychological collapse; Dr. W. Horsley Grant of Johns Hopkins University gives some support to this view by his findings of increased mental disorders in persons who had lived under crowded conditions.[4] Kingsley Davis argues that the impact of giant agglomerations on people "is best indicated by their headlong effort to escape them. The bigger the city, the higher the cost of space; yet, the more the level of living rises, the more people are willing to pay for low-density living. Nevertheless, as urban areas expand and collide, it seems probable that life in low-density surroundings will become too dear for the great majority."[5] Graham Molitor maintains that, "In dense urban-industrial areas, behavioral responses to overcrowding may help explain growing criminal behavior, increasing group disorganization, even the growing incidence of mental disorders."[6] Instead of viewing the urban environment as a luxury he argues that we may need lower densities in order to restore quiet, privacy, independence (mechanisms to relieve system breakdown from overdependence), initiative (constricted by the population crunch), and open space (green belts, recreation areas).

On the other hand, there are those who maintain that experiments with animals should not lead to hasty conclusions concerning human behavior, and that many of the human problems attributed to living in densely-populated areas may be less a result of density than of social factors which happen to be correlated with density. Jean Gottmann, who coined the term *megalopolis*, ventures the opinion

Table 6-1
Proportion of Americans Who Feel That They Reside Under Congested Conditions, 1973

	Congested	Not Particularly Congested	No Response
NATIONWIDE	16	79	5
White	13	83	4
Nonwhite	41	49	10
East	21	73	6
Midwest	15	81	4
South	9	85	6
West	19	78	3
Million and over	28	65	7
500,000-999,999	26	68	6
50,000-499,999	20	75	5
2,500-49,999	10	87	3
Under 2,500	3	94	3

Source: The American Institute of Public Opinion (The Gallup Poll).

Table 6-2
The Relationship Between City Size, Population Density, and Crime Rates in United States Cities

Population Size of Cities in 1960	Average No. People Per Square Mile	Murder	Rape	Robbery	Assault
Over 250,000	7,100	6.8	15.2	117.6	154.1
100,000 to 250,000	4,271	5.6	7.6	56.5	83.3
50,000 to 100,000	3,910	3.3	5.5	36.6	58.9
25,000 to 50,000	2,810	2.9	4.7	22.6	39.9
10,000 to 25,000	2,530	2.4	4.0	15.7	35.2
Under 10,000	1,700	2.7	3.3	12.8	28.9

No. of Crimes Per 100,000 Per Year

Source: Richard D. Lamm, "Local Growth: Focus of a Changing American Value," *Equilibrium,* vol. 1, no. 1 (January 1973), p. 5.

that there is "a certain variety among human beings as to their capacity to live and work at high density. I am convinced that we can perfectly well have very high geographical densities while providing enough privacy for those people who want it."[7] The issue as he sees it is not one of the disorganization of society, but rather its inorganization.

Although the data in Table 6-2 show a clear direct relationship among crime rates, city size, and population density in American cities, care must be taken in their interpretation. For instance, socioeconomic conditions in the ghettos of large cities may well have more to do with crime than density of population. A study prepared for the Commission on Population Growth and the American Future examined the relationship between population density and juvenile delinquency and mental illness in New York City. The results indicated that density, defined either as population per acre or number of people per residential room, is less important than many would believe. There was little or no relationship between density and juvenile delinquency (especially within areas of equal income), but a small, consistent relationship between density and mental illness.[8] More generally, Daniel Stokols recently pointed out that research on human populations indicates that:

spatial restriction is not inevitably associated with social maladies. . . . survey studies, for instance, suggest that in Asian societies cultural traditions serve to offset the detrimental effects of high population density. Experiments concerning the human use of space provide further evidence that cultural norms mediate the perception and adjustment of interpersonal space . . . laboratory investigations of human crowding demonstrate that when group size is held constant and the physical consequences of spatial restriction (for example, high temperature, stuffiness, limited movement) are controlled, high density exerts virtually no ill effects on human task performance. The research on human subjects, then, considered in light of the animal studies, indicates that spatial restriction serves as a necessary antecedent of, but not always a sufficient condition for, the arousal of crowding stress.[9]

Municipal Costs

Apart from questions of the psychological and social-psychological effects of living in big cities, there is the issue of efficiency in the provision of government services. The data in Table 6-3 give the clear overall impression that big cities are inefficient because the cost per capita for most services tends to rise with city size and to be particularly high in the largest size class. However, considerable care should be exercised in interpreting such figures. Do relatively high per-capita outlays in big cities for education, hospitals and health, for example, mean that people in these places are relatively ignorant and in poor health? Or do big cities simply provide better services per capita in these areas? Relatively high police protection expenditures may well reflect higher crime rates in big cities, but it should not be overlooked that many small communities do not report many incidents that go into the crime data in more efficient cities. Though the situation has improved in very recent years, crimes against blacks in the rural and small town South have often escaped official notice. High public welfare outlays in large cities certainly do not reflect a higher incidence of poverty in big cities; while such expenditures are not desirable, they do at least reflect concern with alleviating the distress of the poor, a concern certainly not always found in many nonmetropolitan areas. The fact that per-capita outlays for highways in big cities are about the same as those in other population-size classes would indicate that while it is relatively costly to build highways in big cities, this is compensated for by the more intensive use of them.

Numerous studies of cities in states and regions of the United States have, in fact, turned up conflicting evidence concerning the relationship between population size and municipal costs per capita.[10] The reason may be that some city governments may not operate on the rising portion of the per-capita cost curves associated with various services, but rather open new facilities closer to the locations where the relevant services are demanded.

Foreign evidence concerning the costs associated with various city sizes suggests that intermediate-size cities have certain advantages. G.M. Neutze's analysis of Australian data indicates that most of the advantages of a city of 500,000 inhabitants probably also are found in a city of 200,000, but that if a city gets much beyond the 500,000 level, external diseconomies are likely to begin to outweigh the concomitant economies. He suggests that many firms will maximize their profits in centers with populations between 200,000 and one million.[11] Similarly, in an earlier study, Colin Clark examined structural differences in American, Canadian, and Australian cities of differing sizes and concluded that a city of about 200,00 provides nearly all of the important services and is nearly full-grown with respect to manufacturing at 500,000.[12] A report of the Royal Commission on Local Government in Greater London indicated that the greatest economies of scale occur in the population range from 100,000 to 250,000.[13] Gordon Cameron finds a U-shaped infrastructure cost curve with the minimum cost lying between somewhat less than 30,000 and somewhat more than 250,000.[14] With respect to the

Table 6-3
Per Capita Amounts of Selected City Finance Items by Population-Size Groups Fiscal year 1969

Population Size as of 1960

Item	1,000,000 or More	500,000 to 999,999	300,000 to 499,999	200,000 to 299,999	100,000 to 199,999	50,000 to 99,999	Less Than 50,000
General expenditures, total	411	300	215	192	198	185	120
Education	85	50	41	26	37	36	12
Highways	20	21	18	21	19	19	19
Public welfare	88	25	7	6	7	7	1
Hospitals	35	17	7	2	10	6	5
Health	12	8	3	2	3	2	1
Police protection	44	32	23	21	20	19	14
Fire protection	18	19	16	16	17	16	8
Sewerage	7	13	15	11	9	11	11
Sanitation other than sewerage	15	11	9	9	8	7	5
Parks and recreation	12	17	15	11	11	10	6
Housing and urban renewal	23	15	7	13	12	9	2
Libraries	5	4	4	4	4	3	2
Financial administration	5	5	4	4	3	3	3
General control	9	8	5	5	5	5	5
General public buildings	6	4	2	6	4	4	3
Interest on general debt	15	10	10	10	7	7	5
All other	47	36	30	25	20	21	19
Gross debt outstanding, total	678	399	404	401	307	270	225
Long-term	602	356	361	353	268	238	215
Full faith and credit	400	253	219	199	168	144	92
Utility debt only	153	30	32	22	16	16	16
Nonguaranteed	202	103	142	153	100	95	121
Utility debt only	67	51	66	83	61	55	63
Short-term	76	43	43	49	49	31	10

Source: Richard D. Lamm, "Local Growth: Focus of a Changing American Value," *Equilibrium*, vol. 1, no. 1 (January 1973), p. 5. Data are from U.S. Bureau of the Census.

findings of a research conference sponsored by the International Economic Association, E.A.G. Robinson reports that

> the general sense of our discussions was that the minimum size of growth points that experience had shown to be successful was nearer to a population of 100,000 than to one of 10,000 and that even 100,000 was more likely to be an underestimate than an overestimate. It must be large enough to provide efficiently the main services of education, medical facilities, banking, shopping facilities. . . . Above all, it must be large enough both to provide an efficient infrastructure of public utility services, and to permit the early and progressive growth of external economies for its local industries.[15]

While these examples generally agree that small towns are seldom efficient providers of public services, the results do seem to make a strong case for the intermediate-size city. Nevertheless, it would be a mistake to assume too readily that most big cities are too big. In the present context, the minimizing of per-capita public costs associated with urban size is a poor objective for public policy; economic efficiency would be better served by maximizing the difference between income and costs.

The more general argument can be summarized by reference to William Alonso's aggregate theory of city size.[16] (This section departs from the overall simpler approach taken in this volume and may be skipped by readers without a background in technical economics.) In Alonso's model urban output is the value of the total product of an urban area. Urban costs include quantity and price effects in the costs of public facilities and their operation, in the costs of exogenous inputs other than human ones into the city's economic activity, and in private consumption. Figure 6-1 shows a set of cost and product curves for the city as an aggregate productive unit. The figure is analogous to the usual diagram of costs and revenues for the firm, the key difference being that the horizontal axis shows population rather than quantity produced. The return to labor, here regarded broadly as the total urban population, is the difference between the value of total output and total costs. (Colonial situations in which a part of the output is alienated by others elsewhere are excluded.) The difference between costs and the value of output is available to the city population for investment or direct consumption, either directly from the city's production or through trade with others. The average cost (AC) curve is assumed to rise after a certain population level, even though this may not necessarily be the case.

The average product per-capita (*AP*) curve is linear and increases with population; this simplifies the argument but it also is the form suggested by empirical evidence. The marginal-cost (*MC*) curve shows the extra costs incurred by population growth; so long as *MC* is below the *AC* curve it will keep pulling the average cost down, but once it goes above the *AC* curve the latter will necessarily increase. (The situation is like average and extra scores on examinations. If my exam scores have been increasing lately but are below my average grade, they will still pull down my average grade; once my increasingly high scores go above my grade average, the average will begin to increase.) This means that *MC* intersects *AC* at its minimum point. The relationship between the *MP* and *AP* curves follows similar logic. (So long as my extra exam scores keep increasing, my average grade will keep increasing. There is no downturn in extra scores here, so both *MP* and *AP* increase in linear fashion.)

Given this formulation, it is clear that the point of maximum local contribution to national income occurs at P_c; a national government attempting to maximize total product would have as its target the point where $MC = MP$. The reasoning is simple. At any population less than P_c, an addition to population would add more product than cost, so it would be desirable to expand population. Any additions to population beyond P_c would add more cost than product, so it would not be desirable to go beyond P_c. It is particularly noteworthy that the point of minimum per-capita costs (P_a)—which seems to concern so many writers—is really irrelevant from an efficiency viewpoint.

But what would happen if there were not enough people to push the population of the given city up to the P_c level? What would a national government attempting to maximize total product do? So long as adding people made the difference between *MP* and *MC* in the given city more than it would be in an alternative location, it would expand the population of the given city even if people had to come from other cities. The solution, considering all cities, would be to shuffle population among cities until the difference between *MP* and *MC* was equal everywhere. Otherwise, population could be shifted from where the gains are relatively low to where they are relatively high.

The inhabitants of the city would, however, have a different objective, namely, the maximization of per-capita disposable income, i.e., the difference between *AP* and *AC*. This would occur where the rate of increase of *AP* and *AC* are the same. Because *AP*

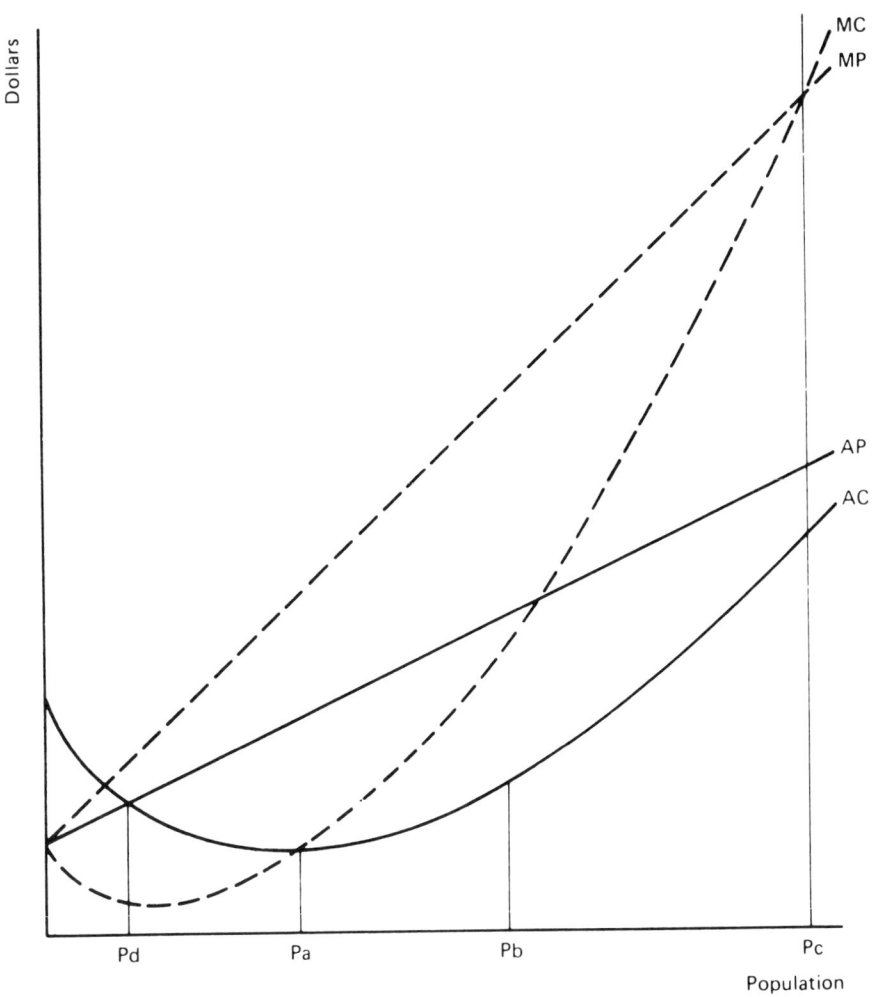

Source: William Alonso, "The Economics of Urban Size," *Papers of the Regional Science Association*, vol. 26 (1971), p. 71.

Figure 6-1. Urban Cost and Product Curves with City Size

increases with population size, this point must lie at a point (P_b) above that where costs are at a minimum. Thus, the point of minimum costs (P_a) does not coincide with the optimal population level from either a national or local viewpoint. The logic that would lead minimum cost theorists to tax new firms on the basis of the difference between social cost, *MC*, and private cost, *AC*, would lead just as well here to a justification for subsidies based on the positive externalities produced by the new arrival. In general, any net tax or subsidy would be based on the difference between $(MP - AP)$, and $(MC - AC)$, which could be positive or negative.

No matter how fine the logic of these arguments, it is not possible at present to quantify operationally the key variables. And even if it were, on the basis of contemporary or historic data, for a given place, it should be recognized that the nature of the curves would change with different time horizon perspectives, which in turn would depend on the adaptability of the urban system. There also is a distributional problem. The marginal product benefits would tend to accrue to the owners of land and other fixed assets, whereas the marginal cost would tend to be borne by others, and particularly by newcomers to the city.

Per-Capita Income

Finally, the argument that income per-capita rises with city size could be interpreted to mean not only that larger cities are more productive, but also that firms that benefit from external economies do so only because they bribe workers to leave smaller (and presumably more satisfying) places by paying higher wages. Wingo points out that if this is the case, it follows that (1) each worker relocates in keeping with his own trade-offs between money and psychological income, and (2) the extra wage required to compensate workers for living in big cities is included in the costs of production in big cities.[17] When the goods and services produced in big cities are sold in the local market, the diseconomies are reflected in a higher cost of living. When they are exported, the purchasers bear the costs of these diseconomies, as they should. The market mechanism thus, in part, reflects the nonmarket costs and benefits of big-city externalities; and to the extent that it does so, it will promote upward pressure on big-city wages or out-migration of workers who give relatively greater weight in their preferences to the nonmonetary psychological income of smaller places.

In spite of the need for much more empirical evidence, there are indications that workers require monetary compensation to offset the negative externalities associated with large cities. Charles Haworth and David Rasmussen recently analyzed differences in the cost of living among metropolitan areas and found that although income does increase with city size, a substantial part of the differential may stem from cost of living differences. They conclude that "any discussion of optimum city size that uses money income will tend to overstate agglomeration economies and understate the relative well-being of nonmetropolitan areas."[18] This conclusion should probably be put this way: Agglomeration economies in large cities enable firms to compensate workers for negative externalities associated with such places, but in themselves they do not provide a sufficient argument in favor of large cities.

George Tolley has put together the results of a number of exploratory studies by other researchers and estimates that wage rates rise more rapidly with city size than do living costs. In his city of one million workers or four million people, an average hourly wage rate of $4.00 contains an extra 5 per cent, or 20 cents an hour, to compensate for negative externalities. In this city, Tolley estimates that the diseconomies of air pollution may be equivalent to 12.5 to 25 cents per working hour, and those of traffic congestion to 6 or 7 cents per working hour. The sum of these figures, 18.5 to 32 cents per working hour, is about the same as the estimated 20 cent margin of wage rates over living costs. This margin may well then be a price paid to big city workers to offset big city negative externalities. Tolley concludes that:

The results suggest the hypothesis that locational effects of externalities impinging on city residents are not negligible, but neither are they so large as to call for the dismantling of cities. A 5 percent increase in the cost of hiring labor would probably make a city grow less rapidly than otherwise, since many labor intensive firms on the margin between locating in the city and elsewhere would then find locations elsewhere more attractive. Since the large cities contain such a preponderance of the population, even a small effect in percentage terms on larger cities would greatly accelerate economic growth in rural areas.[19]

The Size Issue

Wingo also has considered the impact of externalities on firms with different input cost structures, and concludes that there is no reason to believe that externalities necessarily result in cities of larger than optimal size as long as labor and capital are mobile.[20] Moreover, from a national viewpoint, the optimum size of a city can only be defined within the context of the total national settlement pattern.

As pointed out earlier, a small city with proximity to opportunities in large cities is likely to be better off in terms of most economic welfare indices than a city of the same size located in a relatively isolated setting. But then the whole idea of an optimum-size city per se has so few defenders that one wonders why anyone continues to feel an obligation to once more excoriate it.

This is not to deny, however, that a city may be too big (or small) for some purposes. For example, there may well be biases that favor the growth of large cities at the expense of other places. For example, if blue-collar, middle-income workers happen to prefer smaller towns or rural settings, this preference is likely to be negated by union pressures to equalize wages in all places. If wages are subject to national labor contracts, then the location of firms is more likely to be influenced by management's preferences for urban amenities. The fact that an increasing number of managers show willingness to move corporate headquarters from the very largest cities—and especially New York—to other cities still should not provide much comfort for rural development advocates. The losses of the biggest will no doubt be the gain of the big.

Another bias in favor of large-urban areas results from asymmetry in migration. The relatively young and better-educated segments of the nonmetropolitan population tend to move to big cities because of the attractiveness of their employment and life-style alternatives. However, "With time and aging, many come to favor the environment of smaller places, but the elderly tend not to move easily due to heavy sunk investments in homes, friends and local institutions and due also to the shorter remaining life over which the money and psychic cost of moving must be recaptured."[21] By simply not moving, many people in effect choose a larger place as a consequence of the long-run growth of places that once were not large. Thus, there is likely to be a bias in favor of bigness "because those who prefer large cities do tend to act on those preferences and those who prefer smaller places tend not to act. Note also that this age-bias tends to reinforce the 'skill-bias' in migration . . . through which professional and technical workers lock the semi-skilled production workers into their locational preferences for larger urban places."[22]

In spite of these issues, it is still difficult to attribute the problems of big cities to their size as such. Of course, some negative externalities, e.g., congestion and air pollution, may be related to high-density over a significant area. But it is not feasible to attempt to reduce city sizes to correct such externalities. It would be more efficient to take action to eliminate them by prohibitions of noxious activities, taxes, or subsidies for investments in abatement. Moreover, these devices are sufficiently flexible to permit experiments that would be reversible, in contrast to strategies that would reduce city size.

Other urban problems are largely political and social rather than physical; in these instances, *urban structure* rather than *urban size* accounts for many of the disadvantages of large cities.

Thus, in response to the question, "When is a big city too big?" we can only state that from a social point of view we do not know because there are too many complex factors involved in addition to sheer bigness. Nevertheless, urban economics can provide insights into the nature and significance of these factors even if we cannot quantify them precisely. From a personal viewpoint, whether or not a city is too big depends on the preferences of the individual. This still leaves important issues related to urban structure, on which attention will be focused in subsequent chapters.

Urban Growth

A concluding word of caution is, nevertheless, in order concerning the issues of city *size* and city *growth*. Some people want to limit the growth of cities so that they do not become "too big"; they would regard some cities as too big whether or not they are still growing. In contrast, others might emphasize the importance of growth rates rather than size per se. In this context, one might suspend judgment about questions of city size at the large end of the scale, but point out that very rapid growth may be undesirable for cities whether they be big, medium-size, or small.

Employment and population growth well in excess of the national rate implies rapid inmigration, which in turn may lead to deterioration of overburdened public facilities, congestion, housing shortages, and local price inflation. To be sure, many local tradesmen and owners of real estate will benefit from growth and price inflation, but at the expense of transfer payments from others in the local economy. For example, increased rents and land prices do not create *new* wealth or income; they rather reflect the increased scarcity of housing and land in simple supply and demand terms, and those who own the relatively scarce resources gain at the expense of those who do not.

But slow growth, and in some cases decline, of employment and population often results in even more problems than fast growth. It is well known that rural areas, and especially those remote from metropolitan amenities, tend to lose their better trained and educated young people. However, until relatively recently, many such places could count on in-migration and high birth rates to at least maintain the total local population. In fact, in 1950 only two counties in the entire United States had more deaths than births. However, the number increased to 38 in 1960 and then jumped to about 500 in 1970. Again, these counties were overwhelmingly rural in nature and concentrated in the Great Plains, the Corn Belt, central Appalachia, and portions of the southern Coastal Plains. What has happened, of course, is that out-migration has left relatively few people in the age group that forms new families, combined with a relatively large number of older people. In the past, heavy out-migration from rural areas with inadequate opportunities to hold young people contributed significantly to the growth of the cities; today there simply are not enough potential migrants left in rural areas to contribute to the future growth of cities; though there will be exceptions in some regions, the growth of the biggest cities certainly does not owe much to net migration from rural areas, in spite of a great deal of continuing rhetoric to the contrary. As pointed out in Chapter 2, population stagnation and decline are phenomena that have almost invariably been associated with rural areas, but in the future they will characterize many metropolitan areas—and not just their central cities.

Because both very rapid growth and lack of growth are associated with difficult problems of adjustment it is curious that the urban economics literature on desirable rates of city growth is so small in relation to the literature on urban size. In any case, a growth rate approximating that of the nation would appear to be the most desirable unless and until cities are prepared to cope with more extreme situations. Here, too, it is impossible to ignore the internal structure of cities; many, perhaps most, urban problems are related to the fact that the pace and nature of growth has differed among communities within metropolitan areas.

7
The Decline of the Central City

Unlike some Western nations, the United States does not have a national urban-growth policy. Although planners, social scientists, government officials, and others have devoted a great deal of attention to the possible nature and scope of such a policy, there has been little effective political leadership toward this end. However, there has been more enthusiasm for general land-use policy, and an act authorizing federal funds for state land-use planning efforts appears assured of congressional approval at the time of this writing. The debate over this legislation revealed widespread agreement that the greatest opportunities for effective land-use planning and management lie in the rapidly diminishing rural areas of the country, and on the fringe of urban development. With respect to the latter, concern has been voiced that planning and management programs should serve as democratically prepared guides to the future, rather than short-sighted permits to continue the activities of interest groups that have mastered the art of profiting from the "zoning game." Nevertheless, there is a real danger that emphasis on planning "on the fringe of urban development" will neglect critical issues at the heart of the malaise that frequently goes under the label of *urban crisis*. It is very easy to slip from well-intentioned interest in preserving the better qualities of the environment on the fringes to bolstering the interests of those who merely want to preserve their suburban enclaves from invasions from rural areas, or more to the point, the residents of the central cities, many of whom happen to be poor, uncouth, and even black. (It is likely that the reader, like the writer, will be quite aware of this phenomenon by virtue—if that is the correct word—of residence in the suburbs.)

The Central City

Few would quarrel with the notion that areas on the periphery of metropolitan areas should be spared, in so far as possible, the degradations that have accompanied the urban sprawl of the past three decades. Yet, to put too much emphasis on this issue would be to neglect what remains the most critical issue in American urban policy: the decline of the central city. The suburbanization of the national population was noted at the beginning of Chapter 2 (see Table 2-1), because any study of urban growth policy must proceed from this fundamental fact. It also is necessary to recall that in 1970 the proportion of whites who lived in central cities of metropolitan areas was 27.8 per cent, whereas the corresponding figure for blacks was 58.2 per cent. Fully 40.0 per cent of the white population lived in suburban areas, in contrast to only 16.1 per cent of the black population.

Table 7-1 presents data on population change between 1960 and 1970 in the twenty-five largest SMSAs in 1970, and the racial breakdown of percentage population change in their respective central cities. With the exception of Pittsburgh, every one of these SMSAs grew during the decade, but sixteen of the central cities lost population. Even more striking is the fact that while the nonwhite population grew in every central city, the white population declined in eighteen of them. The rate of white population decline in the central city was particularly marked in Washington (39.4 per cent), Newark (36.7 per cent), St. Louis (31.6 per cent), Detroit (29.1 per cent), and Cleveland (26.5 per cent). With the exception of Philadelphia, the central cities that gained white population were all in areas with relatively warm climates and were concentrated in three states: California (Los Angeles, Anaheim, San Diego), Texas (Houston, Dallas) and Florida (Miami). The nonwhite central city growth rate exceeded 50 per cent in eleven SMSAs, and in another nine it was greater than 25 per cent.

The pronounced tendency for the central cities of the largest SMSAs to become increasingly black in racial composition would not be a matter of so much concern were it not for the high incidence of poverty among blacks in these areas. The data in Table 7-2 show that while 7.2 per cent of white families in central cities were in poverty in 1972, this was the case for 27.3 per cent of black families. For unrelated individuals the corresponding values were 24.7 per cent and 37.4 per cent. Still, blacks (and whites) were clearly better off in central cities than in nonmetropolitan areas, where 41.0 per cent of families and 61.3 per cent of unrelated individuals were in poverty. This distinction is also reflected in comparing poverty in the South with that in the rest of the nation. The higher incidence of black poverty in the South is in part attributable to the fact that many southern blacks still live in nonmetropolitan areas with few economic opportunities, whereas the black population in the North is overwhelmingly metropolitan.

It would be a mistake to assume that the problems of metropolitan America boil down to what to do with the black population. Other minorities, including disadvantaged whites, have shared many of the experiences of the blacks. The difficulties of blacks stand out in part because they are by far the largest minority group, and in part because data concerning their social and economic condition are more available and receive greater publicity than is the case for other minorities, e.g., Indians. Nevertheless, it may well be that blacks are more discriminated against than other minorities for a variety of reasons, including status distinctions that go back to the days of slavery, and the simple fact that blacks are usually quite identifiable as such—a fact which increasingly has become a source of pride in an era where the previously undervalued contributions of blacks to American civilization are at last beginning to receive general recognition.

Employment Changes

The plight of the central city poor has been aggravated by the continuing suburbanization of employment opportunities. The data in Table 7-3 show that from 1948 to 1967 suburban areas received nearly 85 per cent of new employment in manufacturing, retail and wholesale trade, and selected services in the 39 SMSAs covered. These SMSAs had a combined 1970 population of about 80.9 million, or 58.5 per cent of the total national metropolitan population. Their black population amounted to 11.4 million, or 67.9 per cent of all metropolitan blacks. Although central cities increased their share of new employment growth between 1963 and 1967, they still managed to capture only a quarter of the total metropolitan increase. During the 1948-67 period the mean annual employment increase in the suburbs was 219,000, compared with only 39,000 in the central cities. Consequently, the central cities' share of total employment in the selected SMSAs fell from 70.6 per cent in 1948 to 54.6 per cent in 1967. At this writing, the proportion is less than half.

Table 7-1
Population Characteristics of the Twenty-Five Largest SMSAs and Their Central Cities

		SMSA Population			Central City Population		
Rank	SMSA	Total, 1970 (thousands)	Net Increase 1960-70 (per cent)	Per Cent of SMSA, 1970	Per Cent Change, 1960-70	Per Cent Change in Whites, 1960-70	Per Cent Change in Nonwhites, 1960-70
1	New York, N.Y.	11,529	7.8	68.2	1.1	−9.3	61.6
2	Los Angeles-Long Beach, Calif.	7,032	16.4	45.1	12.5	4.7	55.6
3	Chicago, Ill.	6,979	12.2	48.2	−5.2	−18.6	38.4
4	Philadelphia, Pa.-N.J.	4,818	10.9	40.4	−2.7	12.9	25.2
5	Detroit, Mich.	4,200	11.6	36.0	−9.5	−29.1	38.1
6	San Francisco-Oakland, Calif.	3,110	17.4	34.6	−2.8	−17.2	51.3
7	Washington, D.C.-Md.-Va.	2,861	38.6	26.4	−1.0	−39.4	30.7
8	Boston, Mass.	2,754	6.1	23.3	−8.1	−16.5	69.9
9	Pittsburgh, Pa.	2,401	−0.2	21.7	−13.9	−18.0	6.0
10	St. Louis, Mo.-Ill.	2,363	12.3	26.3	−17.0	−31.6	19.1

11	Baltimore, Md.	2,071	14.8	43.7	−3.5	−21.4	29.7
12	Cleveland, Oh.	2,064	8.1	36.4	−14.3	−26.5	15.7
13	Houston, Tex.	1,985	40.0	62.1	31.4	25.5	50.9
14	Newark, N.J.	1,857	9.9	20.6	−5.6	−36.7	53.6
15	Minneapolis-St. Paul, Minn.	1,814	22.4	41.0	−6.1	−7.9	49.8
16	Dallas, Tex.	1,556	39.1	54.3	24.2	14.2	66.3
17	Seattle-Everett, Wash.	1,422	28.5	41.1	−4.4	−8.5	43.5
18	Anaheim-Santa Ana-Garden Grove, Calif.	1,420	101.8	31.4	54.4	50.8	301.6
19	Milwaukee, Wis.	1,404	9.8	51.1	−3.3	−10.4	69.9
20	Atlanta, Ga.	1,390	36.7	35.7	2.0	−20.0	37.3
21	Cincinnati, Oh.-Ky.-Ind.	1,385	9.2	32.7	−10.0	−17.2	15.9
22	Paterson-Clifton-Passaic, N.J.	1,359	14.5	20.8	1.0	−9.1	98.1
23	San Diego, Calif.	1,358	31.4	51.3	21.6	17.2	72.8
24	Buffalo, N.Y.	1,349	3.2	34.3	−13.1	−20.7	34.1
25	Miami, Fla.	1,268	35.6	26.4	14.8	13.5	19.3

Source: U.S. Bureau of the Census, *Statistical Abstract of the United States: 1972* (Washington, D.C.: U.S. Government Printing Office, 1972). pp. 838-81.

Table 7-2
Families and Unrelated Individuals Below the Poverty Level in 1972, by Place of Residence, Region and Race of Head (numbers in thousands; families and unrelated individuals as of March 1973)

	All races			White			Black		
		Below Low-Income Level			Below Low-Income Level			Below Low-Income Level	
	Total	Number	Per Cent	Total	Number	Per Cent	Total	Number	Per Cent
FAMILIES									
United States	54,373	5,075	9.3	48,477	3,441	7.1	5,265	1,529	29.0
Metropolitan areas[a]	36,941	2,938	8.0	32,303	1,819	5.6	4,117	1,059	25.7
Inside central cities	16,159	1,828	11.3	12,595	901	7.2	3,263	892	27.3
Outside central cities	20,782	1,110	5.3	19,708	918	4.7	854	167	19.5
Nonmetropolitan areas[a]	17,433	2,137	12.3	16,174	1,622	10.0	1,148	471	41.0
North and West	37,098	2,761	7.4	33,968	2,091	6.2	2,589	598	23.1
South	17,275	2,314	13.4	14,508	1,350	9.3	2,676	931	34.8
UNRELATED INDIVIDUALS									
United States	16,811	4,883	29.0	14,495	3,935	27.1	2,028	870	42.9
Metropolitan areas[a]	12,182	3,139	25.8	10,308	2,447	23.7	1,629	625	38.4
Inside central cities	7,293	1,977	27.1	5,781	1,429	24.7	1,330	498	37.4
Outside central cities	4,889	1,161	23.7	4,527	1,018	22.5	299	127	42.6
Nonmetropolitan areas[a]	4,629	1,745	37.7	4,187	1,488	35.5	399	244	61.3
North and West	12,156	3,246	26.7	10,832	2,792	25.8	1,072	380	35.5
South	4,655	1,637	35.2	3,663	1,143	31.2	956	489	51.2

[a]Based on SMSAs as defined in the 1970 census.

Source: Current Population Reports, *Consumer Income, Characteristics of the Low-Income Population: 1972.* Series P-60, no. 88, June 1973 (Washington, D.C.: U.S. Government Printing Office, 1973), p. 7.

Table 7-3
Employment[a] Changes in 39 Selected SMSAs, Central Cities, and Suburbs, 1948, 1963, 1967

Category	SMSA	Central City	Suburban Ring
Net increase in employment			
1948-67	5,151,000	782,000	4,369,000
1963-67	2,136,000	542,000	1,594,000
Percentage distribution of new employment			
1948-67	100	15.1	84.9
1963-67	100	24.4	74.6
Mean annual increase in employment			
1948-67	258,000	39,000	219,000
1963-67	534,000	136,000	398,000
Mean annual percentage increase in employment			
1948-67	2.1	0.9	5.9
Percent of total SMSA employment			
1948	100	70.6	29.4
1967	100	54.6	45.4

[a]Refers to employment in manufacturing, retail, and wholesale trade, and selected services.

Source: Neil N. Gold, "The Mismatch of Jobs and Low-Income People in Metropolitan Areas and its Implications for the Central City Poor," U.S. Commission on Population Growth and the American Future, *Population Distribution and Policy,* Sara Mills Mazie, ed., vol. V of Commission research reports (Washington, D.C.: U.S. Government Printing Office, 1972). The data were compiled from *Census of Manufacturing* and *Census of Business*, 1948, 1954, 1958, 1963, 1967.

Bureau of the Census estimates of occupational employment changes in SMSAs indicate that jobs suitable to the skill levels of the central-city poor, and particularly the male poor, are declining or else growing only slightly in central cities, while expanding at a rapid pace in the suburbs. In contrast, the new jobs that are being created in the central cities are not well suited to the occupational requirements of the central-city poor, though they are appropriate for commuters from the suburbs. The data in Table 7-4 indicate that male employment in central cities actually declined by 2 per cent between 1960 and 1970. Meanwhile, jobs for males and females increased substantially in the suburbs.

Almost four out of five new jobs held by central-city males were in the highly skilled professional and managerial category. Male employment in the clerical and sales and operatives categories

Table 7-4
Employment Changes Among Civilians 14 Years and Over by Selected Nonfarm Occupation Groups 1960-70[a] (in thousands)

Occupation	Metropolitan Areas Net Increase	Metropolitan Areas Per Cent Increase	Central Cities Net Increase	Central Cities Per Cent Increase	Suburbs Net Increase	Suburbs Per Cent Increase
Male						
Total	4,390	16.0	−280	−2.0	4,670	35.4
Professional and managerial	3,350	51.4	610	19.3	2,740	81.3
Clerical and sales	440	9.6	−130	−5.1	570	26.8
Craftsmen and foremen	790	13.9	20	1.1	770	25.1
Operatives	540	9.8	−60	−2.1	600	23.1
Other service workers	450	23.7	120	9.9	330	46.9
Nonfarm laborers	310	16.9	90	8.9	220	26.6
Female						
Total	5,780	41.2	1,451	17.5	4,418	74.4
Professional and managerial	1,640	69.7	540	41.2	1,100	105.3
Clerical and sales	3,090	52.8	960	28.9	2,130	84.5
Craftsmen and foremen	40	21.7	10	8.6	30	38.6
Operatives	430	20.2	20	1.8	410	46.4
Private household workers	200	20.0	−90	−14.6	290	83.0
Other service workers	1,360	76.4	600	58.3	760	101.1

[a]1960 data from Census of Population and Housing; 1970 data from Current Population Survey.

Source: Neil N. Gold, "The Mismatch of Jobs and Low-Income People in Metropolitan Areas and its Implications for the Central City Poor," U.S. Commission on Population Growth and the American Future, *Population Distribution and Policy*, Sara Mills Mazie, ed., vol. V of Commission research reports (Washington, D.C.: U.S. Government Printing Office, 1972). The data were compiled from U.S. Bureau of the Census, *Current Population Survey*.

Note: Number may not add to totals because of rounding and occupations not reported.

—semiskilled and low-skilled for the most part—declined in central cities during the 1960s. The number of male craftsmen, service workers, and laborers rose only slightly. Central-city female clerical and sales and other service worker jobs increased substantially. Although suburban employment increased sharply in all occupational categories among both male and female workers, the most notable gains were in the clerical and sales, craftsmen and foremen, and operatives categories, all of which are suitable for semiskilled and low-skilled workers. The general picture, then, is one of a severe geographical imbalance between residences and work places in metropolitan areas. The suburbanization of semiskilled and low-skilled jobs has grave implications for central cities and especially the minority poor. Moreover, there is little evidence to believe that the decentralization of jobs will be reversed. Rather, it appears likely that the minority poor and unskilled will continue to be relegated to older central-city housing, distant from expanding suburban employment centers. The reasons for this phenomenon are complex. Yet, as Neil Gold points out:

there can be no question that the urban poor—particularly the minority poor—are being excluded from suburban housing markets, and that this exclusion is accomplished through a combination of private and public actions, through acts of both omission and commission. Nearly 80 percent of the public housing units constructed in metropolitan areas in the middle 1960's, for example, have been located in the central cities, compared with only one-third of new private housing units. Conversely, two out of three private housing units, but only one out of five public housing units were constructed in the suburbs in these years. To the extent that this phenomenon is nonracial, it results from the interaction of state and national land-use policies with antiquated mercantilist fiscal structures at the local level, which pit community against community in a race to secure high-value ratables and to exclude low- and moderate-income housing.

Unless these barriers can be overcome to bring the urban poor into greater physical proximity with new employment growth on the urban fringe, through metropolitan-wide dispersal of low- and moderate-income housing and/or through the provision of appropriate transportation linkages between residences and work places, sub-employment among the urban poor is likely to increase in the coming years, with adverse effects on fiscal conditions and on intergroup tensions in central cities. Without enforcement of the civil rights laws, however, even these strategies will fail to bring about equal employment opportunity for the minority poor in metropolitan areas.[1]

The process by which central-city residents have been divorced from suburban employment opportunities is clearly complex, but its principal elements are identifiable. In Chapter 5 it was argued that close proximity, with its concomitant externalities, is the essential attribute of cities. For this reason the city's transportation-communication system is perhaps the most important single determinant of the urban process. If positive externalities are to be realized, the friction of distance must be overcome. Without change in the transportation system the only way to accommodate more people is by large increases in settlement density. This results in very high construction costs and enables people to consume only very small amounts of land. Expansion of the transportation system or a shift to new technologies, as from streetcars to autos, opens up new territory so that more people can have the same access without incurring the crowding and construction costs of higher density.[2]

Transportation

In early industrial centers, workers were grouped in housing close to their places of work. Even employers did not commute long distances but more often drove to work in carriages from houses within convenient reach of their factories. Contemporary urban transportation systems and traffic conditions owe almost as much to improved standards of living as to the growth of cities. The choice of both residence and mode of travel has been affected by expectations of greater comfort and convenience, as well as the ability to pay higher costs. The transportation problems of cities have thus been brought about by people themselves taking advantage of individual opportunities.[3] As a reflection of the post-World War II pattern of living, the total number of passenger trips by mass transit facilities has declined in every year since the war. Much of the early postwar decline resulted from abnormal wartime conditions, when restrictions on automobile use caused many people to shift to mass transit. In fact, mass-transit patronage was about the same in 1953 as in 1941. Today, however, it is only about two-thirds of what it was in those years, in spite of considerable growth in urban population. This is explained by steadily expanding auto ownership. In 1950 six in every 10 U.S. households owned one or more private autos. By 1967 the corresponding figure was nearly eight in 10. However, among families with before-tax income between $2,000 and $2,999, the ownership rate in 1967 was only 53 per cent. The proportion of households owning autos in the below-$2,000 group is much lower. Moreover, when they do own autos, poor people generally own poor ones that often are not adequate for long-distance commuting and expressway use. The urban poor thus continue to depend heavily on public transportation. Increasingly, poor workers are compelled to choose between a higher paying job that cannot be reached by public transportation, and thereby pay more for transportation by buying and operating an auto, or a lower paying job that is served by mass transit.[4]

Some would argue that in an age when the automobile has become almost an end in itself, the suburbanite and the central-city resident are both victims. Thus, Bennett Harrison maintains that:

Places like Los Angeles depend crucially on the private car. But that dependence is not "natural"; it is the result of decades of public policy. It hardly needs demonstrating here that government policy discriminates in favor of the auto and against any other form of transportation. Each year, the United States spends ten times as much on highway construction as on mass transportation. That this need not be is clear to anyone who has seen the quality of mass transit in other industrial societies. Thus it makes little sense to say that Americans "prefer" to do all their traveling by auto. In the suburbs, at least, they have no choice in the matter: the car is the only means of transport available to them, and hardly any place is within walking distance.[5]

Harrison's implication that government policy has been out of tune with people's preferences may not be true. Nevertheless, if major changes are to be made in present systems of transportation, deliberate individual and collective choices must first be made concerning the more general issue of the quality of urban life, and the equitability of the distribution of opportunities in the urban system. Transportation policies can help create new, more satisfying urban settlements or they can have the contrary effect. Transportation technology makes possible a wide range of choices, but the choices themselves must be deliberate acts of public policy. (The choice of the word "must" here may be inappropriate in view of the considerable evidence that public policy may have, and indeed often has had, a distinctly accidental quality.) The issue for public policy-makers is how to increase access and to make access serve in the attainment of urban goals. "This is not the same as the familiar preoccupation with getting the largest number of people moved between two points at the lowest possible cost. Transportation is the means by which a whole city functions and human aspirations are furthered. The freedom to move will determine whether or not it will be possible to participate in the activity and diversity of the city."[6]

There is substantial general agreement that simply giving larger subsidies to urban mass-transit systems is not likely to be an effective means for increasing the mobility of the central city poor. The transportation demands involved in getting central-city workers to outlying work places are too complex to be met adequately at costs that are competitive with private autos. New systems are needed and there is some agreement on their nature. They would use a smaller vehicle than conventional mass transit, would be demand-activated rather than operated on fixed routes and schedules, and would provide or at least approximate point-to-point service. Such systems would probably have somewhat lower passenger mile costs than taxis, but unit costs would probably be somewhat higher than those of current mass-transit systems. In some cases, the new services might supplement the more heavily-used existing public transportation system, but in other cases, they might replace the latter altogether.[7]

One proposed innovation in providing more effective transportation for the poor is to rent, lease, or otherwise finance new or relatively new cars for low-income households. However, if this "new Volks for poor folks" approach is to be feasible, the cost of credit must be lowered. A similar proposal is to assist central-city residents who work in the suburbs to sell transportation services to fellow workers to help pay for the purchase and operating costs of the auto. (The energy crisis that hit an unsuspecting public in 1973 might make this proposal attractive to even broader segments of the population.) Unfortunately, new autos for poor people will not help nondrivers, who now account for an estimated 20 percent of all persons over 17 years of age. Demand actuated systems going under a variety of names (Taxi-bus, Dial-a-bus) have been suggested to provide mobility for nondrivers. The basic idea is at least to approximate the point-to-point service of taxis while achieving better utilization levels and load factors than mass transit vehicles now realize on fixed routes and schedules. It is claimed that electronic control and scheduling can assemble loads with a minimum of delay. The costs of such service would, like the size of vehicles involved, be intermediate to the conventional taxi and bus. Demand-actuated systems might be particularly helpful to the elderly and infirm; and they might be a more politically acceptable alternative than the extension of ownership of private autos, especially in older cities with high-population density in central-city neighborhoods. Ownership of these systems might vary from place to place and over periods of time. Elaborate control and scheduling might require a fleet of vehicles, but in other cases, service might be provided by large numbers of owner-operators working independently or in a cooperative arrangement. These proposals fortunately lend themselves to relatively modest experimentation before any major policy commitments need be made.[8]

Housing

Although improved transportation would help give central-city residents better opportunities to reach suburban jobs, an even more fundamental problem is housing discrimination. Indeed, if it were not for housing discrimination, the need to improve central-city access to the suburbs through better transportation would not be so pressing. It has been estimated that in 1968 the suburbs housed 45 per cent of the urban white poor, but only 23 per cent of the urban nonwhite poor. The clear inference is that poverty alone does not deny access to suburban residences to the nonwhite poor.[9] Moreover, the lack of an open-housing market and the urban system's unresponsiveness to the demand for low-income housing in the suburbs—especially for blacks—has been exacerbated by the difficulty of expanding the housing supply in the central city. There is abundant evidence that the supply of low-income housing is less than elastic and that it is locationally fixed by the prevailing pattern of housing stock available as well as the existence of a strong social contiguity constraint. The difficulty of expanding the housing supply in the central city means that poor-quality housing is relatively high-priced and often more profitable for property owners than would be expected under true market-equilibrium conditions.[10]

John Kain has pointed out that there are several reasons why housing market segregation may affect the distribution and level of black employment. First, the difficulty of reaching many jobs from black areas may impose costs that discourage blacks from taking them. Second, blacks may have less information and less opportunity to learn about relatively distant employment opportunities. Third, employers located outside the ghetto may discriminate against blacks because of real or imagined fears of retaliation from white customers for bringing blacks into white residential areas, or they may feel little pressure not to discriminate. And finally, employers in or near the ghetto may discriminate in favor of blacks. Kain used data from Detroit and Chicago to test the hypothesis that housing market discrimination reduces black employment, and his results suggested that job losses in this respect could be as large as 24,600 in Chicago and 9,100 in Detroit.[11] In spite of some controversy concerning Kain's findings, more recent evidence supports or else fails to refute his principal conclusions.[12] Although there are still glaring inadequacies in our understanding of the ways in which housing markets and labor markets are interrelated, and especially of the ways in which housing market discrimination affects these markets, the present state of knowledge indicates that: "The effect of housing market discrimination on Negro welfare extends well beyond the employment effects. . . . Indeed, the welfare losses experienced by Negro households in housing, education, and other areas may be larger and have greater long range significance. Moreover, not all of the costs of discrimination are borne by Negro Americans. . . . housing market segregation imposes large costs on centrally employed whites, has created major distortions in the patterns of metropolitan growth, and bears a major responsibility for a surprisingly long list of urban ills."[13]

Tax Policies

The "balkanization" of metropolitan areas and the related issue of tax policies represent still other forces acting to undermine the viability of central cities. New political jurisdictions usually come into being by the formation of incorporations at the edges of settlement. Since they offer an opportunity for people to segregate themselves into separate taxing areas, it is not surprising that they would do so in ways that tend to exclude people with lower incomes or greater desires for government services. In this process people are given a chance to trade somewhat poorer access for a better individual buy in public services, but historically the increased costs of a more remote location have tended to be subsidized through heavy transportation investments financed for the most part by the metropolitan area as a whole or by the state and federal governments.[14]

It has been argued that there are certain advantages to political fragmentation because it permits people with differing tastes for public goods to accommodate these differences, instead of everyone in the metropolis having to consume a standard package. Charles Tiebout has developed a well-known model in which each prospective consumer-resident shops around the metropolis until he finds a community offering a tax and expenditure package that corresponds to his own preferences. He then "votes with his feet" by moving into this community.[15] While there is limited empirical evidence suggesting that consumer-residents do balance public services against taxes in choosing a location,[16] many other factors also are involved. For example, information about public services and taxes is never perfect, and capital flows within the metropolitan area may reduce the extent to which a favorable tax-expenditure package is capitalized into land values. Even more important in the present context, "unfortunately the ability of individuals to take advantage of such possibilities varies directly with their income and attempts to finance local services on either a benefit or an ability-to-pay principle are severely frustrated. In any case, it is clear that the present rules for the organization of political jurisdictions do affect the changing form of the metropolis."[17] In more general terms, Bennett Harrison maintains that:

Suburban residents are subsidized at the expense of city residents. Federal tax deductions for mortgage interest and property taxes provide a massive subsidy for homeowners, who are mostly suburban; tenants, who are mostly urban, are denied that subsidy. Because local government depends mainly on the local property tax, and because the poor are concentrated in the core, city taxpayers bear the burden of services for the poor. The suburbs, which zone out the poor, escape that burden. Thus Americans who choose the suburbs need not be expressing a preference for suburban over city living as such. They may simply be recognizing that public policy rewards them for living in the other. In fact, research shows that most white migrants to the suburbs are responding to these tax pressures rather than to racial mixture or fear of crime in the cities. In these circumstances, it is remarkable that so many people are willing to pay the price to live in cities.[18]

Roy Bahl similarly points out that the ideal solution of the Tiebout model is impeded by central city-suburb fiscal imbalances. "The catalyst of the metropolitan fiscal problem is the secular industrial and residential movement which has simultaneously depleted the central city tax base and forced on the core city government the dual responsibilities of serving a high-cost, low-income population (much of which is elderly, poor, and/or black) and meeting the needs of a sizable commuter population."[19] The fiscal-disparity problem, moreover, is not simply the existence of a resources-requirements gap for a particular local government or for the SMSA as a whole. It is, rather, variations in the size of the gap among communities within the SMSA. If outlays exceeded receipts by the same per-capita amount in each community (given a constant fiscal effort), or if there were a single metropolitan government, the problem would not exist. Moreover, not only are there considerable disparities among communities—the central city is in the most unfavorable position in nearly all cases.

Sacks and Campbell, using 1964-65 data for the nation's 37 largest SMSAs, found that per-capita total taxes were higher in central cities than in suburbs. Although per-capita property tax levels were about the same, there was evidence from previous work that effective rates were significantly greater in central cities. Central-city governments spent more for direct-benefit (noneducational) services than did suburban governments, but the latter spent a proportionately greater amount for education. Locally-financed education outlays were $14.19 per capita higher in the suburbs; the inclusion of federal and state aid increased this difference to $24.82. The converse was true for noneducational outlays, which include heavily aided welfare, highway, housing, and urban-development programs.[20]

Sacks' analysis of more recent data (see Table 7-5) suggests that the relative position of the central cities has worsened. It should be noted that median family income is about 20 percent greater outside central cities, and this may be an understatement because the suburban figure includes some rural areas on the metropolitan fringe. From a smaller resource base a greater per-capita level of taxes is extracted in the central cities. However, tax effort, as measured by the ratio of taxes to income, may be relatively overstated in the central cities because their larger nonresidential component suggests greater opportunity to "export" the tax. Given these caveats, the data in Table 7-5 indicate that only with respect to per-capita noneducational expenditures and intergovernmental aid do the central cities seem to be in a stronger position than the suburbs. However, the higher per-capita noneducational outlays (which receive a higher level of aid to central cities) do not necessarily imply correspondingly high-service levels in the cities, because they also are demanded by nonresident commuters. The data also suggest that in a Tiebout sense "the core city in the metropolitan area offers the consumer-resident at least a relatively lower quality package of education services at a relatively higher cost. Such a public service package is unlikely to bid middle and upper income families to the core city, or to keep them there."[21] In addition, comparable data over time for 25 SMSAs give little evidence that the nonproperty tax base is increasing in central cities. Growth rates in retail sales, employment, and personal income are all lower in central cities than in their suburbs.[22]

To make matters even more difficult, the central cities' renewal is often impeded by the property tax. If they are taxed according to their current market worth, new well-constructed buildings are taxed more heavily than slum property. An increased property tax can represent a cost for which the owner receives no corresponding increase in government services; and this in spite of the fact that high-quality buildings bring the general public some positive externalities. Thus, although no one intentionally created a tax system that would favor holding decrepit buildings while penalizing new ones, the property tax in fact discourages investors from putting funds into the new and the good. It similarly discourages maintenance and modernization. The property tax may also cause homeowners to lose more benefits than simply the money paid to the government. By increasing the price of housing, this tax creates pressure for building smaller units—yet, construction costs per cubic foot decrease with size of structure. Yet another problem arises from the variation in property tax rates among communities. A few areas may get by as "islands" with low tax rates, thereby attracting capital for new structures. Lower tax rates on the metropolitan fringe encourage dispersal of activities that would be more economically located in closer proximity to other activities; the bias in favor of horizontal rather than vertical growth imposes higher real costs in terms of time and money in travel and higher expenses for water supply and sewage and garbage disposal.[23]

The way to eliminate the perverse effects of property taxation would be to make land the tax base, and put less burden on buildings, equipment, and inventories. The tax might also be related more to

Table 7-5
Central City-Suburb Disparities for 37 Largest Metropolitan Areas in 1968

	Central City	Outside Central City	Metropolitan Area
Per capita total expenditures	$ 408	$ 332	$ 367
Per capita educational expenditures	137	178	158
Per capita noneducational expenditures	271	158	220
Per capita taxes	226	173	198
Per capita aid	133	99	...
Taxes as per cent of income	6.3%	4.2%	...
Median family income	$8,616	$10,769	$9,923

Source: Seymour Sacks, "Fiscal Disparities and Metropolitan Development," in *Papers Submitted to Subcommittee on Housing Panels on Housing Production, Housing Demand, and Developing a Suitable Living Environment*, Part 2 (Washington: U.S. Government Printing Office, 1971). Cited in Roy W. Bahl, "Metropolitan Fiscal Structures and the Distribution of Population within Metropolitan Areas," in U.S. Commission on Population Growth and the American Future, *Population Distribution and Policy*, Sara Mills Mazie, ed., vol. V of Commission research reports (Washington, D.C.: U.S. Government Printing Office), p. 429.

the costs of providing services such as streets, sewers, and fire protection. In view of the rationing function of prices, a high price for some land is essential to encourage its best use. But efficiency only requires that the user pay the price (presumably he can bid higher than other potential users because he can put it to more remunerative use); it does not mean that the owner receive more. Because land is fixed in supply the government can tax the owner's rent without affecting the supply. It is even possible that more land would become available for use as owners seek to obtain the best possible income from land that costs more simply to hold. At the same time, lowering the tax on improvements would increase the attractiveness of investment in newer and better buildings and equipment. To be sure, slums would not be replaced by more modern structures immediately, but the process of replacement would be accelerated. More intensive use of central cities would result, and the filling-in of idle land and upgrading of older areas would be accompanied by more vertical development of better facilities. The reduced incentive for urban sprawl would in effect mean that elevators would play a greater role in transportation and autos less.

Of course, increasing the tax on the basis of the existing value of land would work against present land owners, but there seems little justification in granting tax favoritism to those who withhold land from its optimum use. Also, much of what people are willing to pay for the use of a given piece of land reflects social investment in streets, schools, and other facilities. The community can certainly legitimately recoup in taxes some of the value it has created.[24]

In sum, there are a number of fiscal measures that could be used to improve fiscal imbalances and induce middle- and high-income individuals and families to choose central-city locations. It should be noted, however, that these measures would not necessarily induce low-income central-city residents to choose suburban locations, or make them more able to do so; taxation policy changes will not substitute for reforms in the areas of improved transportation, zoning, and open housing enforcement. Possible fiscal reforms are the following:

1. The adoption of metropolitan areawide taxes, with the proceeds distributed within the metropolitan area on a basis of fiscal capacity and expenditure needs. Such taxes would replace a part of the property tax.
2. A higher percentage deduction of local taxes and perhaps mortgage interest payments from the federal income tax for central city than for suburban residents. For example, a city resident might be allowed to deduct total local tax payments and mortgage interest charges, whereas a suburban resident could deduct only 50 percent of the total.
3. Revamping of tax structures on a case-by-case basis in central cities so as to promote redevelopment. The exemption of improvements from property taxes for a period of years, and differentially lower rates on improvements thereafter, might be one acceptable formula.
4. State or federal assumption of full financial responsibility for the welfare function in the 16 states where it is still partly a local function.
5. State assumption of major financial responsibility for education through a state education grant-in-aid system that truly reflects both need and fiscal capacity differentials.
6. The development of a state government unconditional (noneducation) grants program with proceeds distributed on a needs and

capacity basis. Objective needs measures could be developed. This program and the education grants program described above would be the main vehicles by which shared federal revenues would be passed through.[25]

Although this listing involves piecemeal measures, this does not deny that metropolitan goals might best be served by a single integrated and consistent program for reducing disparities. Moreover, it would seem that state governments are in the best position to deliver such programs.

Regional Exceptions

In closing, it should be remarked that the stereotyped dichotomy between a central city where most of the social and economic problems of a metropolitan area are found, and a healthy, happy suburbia where most problems are merely a result of growing pains, is by no means a universal phenomenon. Marjorie Cahn Brazer analyzed the structure of all SMSAs with populations over 100,000 in terms of 41 variables measuring such characteristics as nonwhite population, age, mobility, families with children under 18 years of age, unrelated individuals, education, occupation, women in the labor force, family income, unemployment, substandard housing, and commuters. For only three of the 41 variables—race, broken families with children, and unrelated individuals—is a metropolitan dichotomy indisputable and pervasive. In many metropolitan areas of the South and West and in smaller SMSAs throughout the nation, low-status nonwhites make up a larger proportion of the suburban population than of the central city population. Substandard owner-occupied housing also is more prevalent in the suburbs everywhere except in the Northeast. For the country as a whole "the cities and suburbs of most metropolitan areas face similar social problems and by and large enjoy similar human and personal economic resources with which to meet these problems."[26] Nevertheless, in the Northeast and in most of the largest SMSAs elsewhere, the central city-suburb dichotomy is marked and at least approximates the stereotype. These SMSAs are numerically in the minority but they account for most of the total metropolitan population. Of the 190 SMSAs studied by Brazer, 41 were in the Northeast; those in the rest of the nation with over one million population numbered only 17. In most of the remaining SMSAs the areas as a whole share similar problems and should recognize the advantages of intrametropolitan cooperation in dealing with them.[27]

The South

In this context the South deserves special consideration. Figure 7-1 shows the per cent change in urban population by state between 1960 and 1970. Among the states of the Confederacy, only Louisiana and Alabama had urban growth rates below the national average of 19.2 per cent. And Alabama's 12 per cent figure—the lowest in the South—still was greater than that in 12 other states. Yet, of the 25 largest SMSAs in 1970 (see Table 7-1), only four were in the South, and three of these—Houston, Dallas, and Miami—are located in areas very peripheral to the more densely settled areas of the Confederacy. But by any measure, the urbanization of the South is based on the rapid growth of small- and medium-size metropolitan areas.

A recent review of 16 state and national surveys of community-size preferences included only one survey limited to the South, and it concerned only North Carolina. Although there were problems of varying definitions in the surveys, the review found that preference for metropolitan living was the least in the North Carolina case.[28] This is not inconsistent with the location preference data reported in Chapter 3. It also is in accord with the responses of a sample of 385 persons in two North Carolina Piedmont cities—Durham (1970 population, 95,438) and Greensboro (144,076)—who were interviewed to gain some understanding of how they felt about their cities. Eighty-one per cent of the Durham respondents and 82 per cent of the Greensboro respondents indicated that they were either satisfied or very much satisfied. Only 3 per cent of the Durham sample and 4 per cent of the Greensboro sample indicated any dissatisfaction with their cities. The respondents were also asked the question, "If you had complete freedom to choose the size of city in which you would live, which of these city sizes would be your first choice?" (A card was presented listing examples of Southern cities in various population categories.) For both cities combined, 60 per cent preferred a city in the 10,000-100,000 population range, and

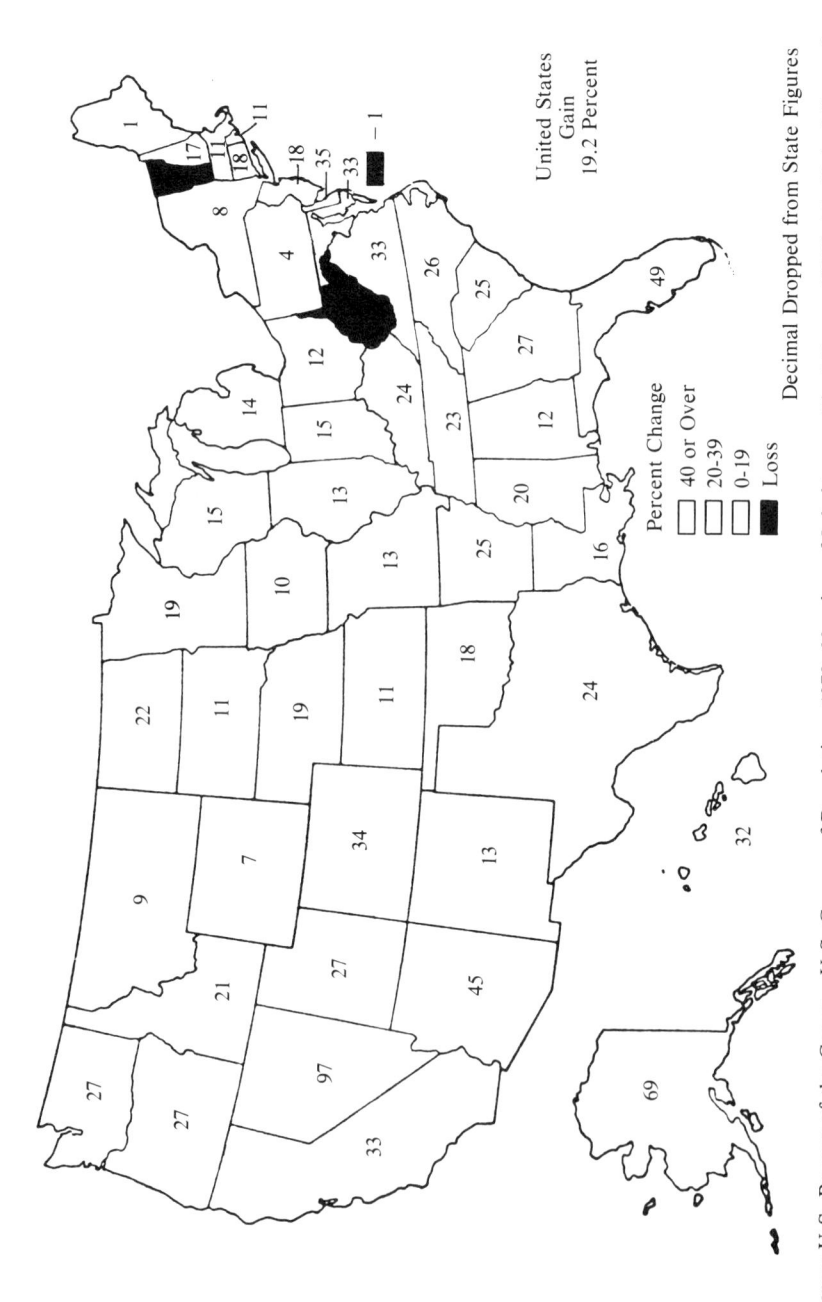

Figure 7-1. Per Cent of Change in Urban Population by States: 1960 to 1970

Source: U.S. Bureau of the Census, U.S. Census of Population: 1970, *Number of Inhabitants*, Final Report PC(1)-A1, United States Summary (Washington, D.C.: U.S. Government Printing Office, 1971), p. 31.

another 9 per cent preferred a city in the 100,000-500,000 range. Only 6 per cent would prefer to live in a metropolitan city with over 500,000 people. The satisfaction of the respondents with their environment was also tested, using responses to photographs of various types of residential areas. This study showed that people do have preferences and are able to recognize gradations of beauty, convenience, and other qualities that can be affected by urban planning.[29] If the Crescent cities did not fulfill the full range of livability preferences of the majority of respondents, it was equally clear that "there is a greater challenge in meeting needs on a much larger scale elsewhere where urban agglomerations have lost many of the living qualities the Crescent cities still possess."[30] It is noteworthy in the present context that a related study showed that migrants to Durham and Greensboro had achieved a reasonably contented existence. In this respect these cities were considered representative of other cities in the Piedmont Crescent. Adjustment of the newcomers was aided by the fact that most were natives of the Southeast, and many were able to maintain frequent contacts with friends and relatives in the areas from which they moved.[31]

Although these findings may not typify the entire South, my own experience working in the region leads me to believe that they are fairly representative. Over 40 years ago Rupert Vance envisioned a pattern of urbanization for the South that still has appeal:

While the South develops the small city, the medium city, and a few large cities, it need not produce the metropolis. Thus, it may avoid traffic congestion, the creation of slum areas, the loss of time going to and from work, and the corrupt and inefficient municipal housekeeping almost invariably attached to overdeveloped population centers. If such a program is possible, the South may finally attain many of the advantages of contemporary industrialization without suffering its accompanying deficiencies and maladjustments.[32]

One may argue whether or not the "corrupt and inefficient" metropolis could have learned much virtue from southern towns. Also, the industrialization of the South is more a rural and small-town phenomenon than one pertaining to the region's metropolitan areas. From the viewpoint of the metropolitan areas, this need not cause alarm in an age when the dominant and most rapidly growing activities are in the tertiary sector. Nevertheless, the cities of the South (and to a somewhat less degree, the West) have options that Northern cities long ago gave up.

In spite of the persistence of traditional barriers to progress, there are at work in the South and in the South's interrelations with the rest of the nation a number of positive forces. These include relatively rapid urbanization, increasing integration of southern economic and social life with that of the rest of the nation, the emergence of younger political leaders with the courage to deal constructively with racial problems, and a growing realization in the North that southern problems are in many respects national in scope and should be treated from that perspective. There are those who believe that the South will—not least through its handling of the urbanization process—in the long run reconcile the races in a more profound way than the North. Whether or not this will be the case, it is a worthy goal from an economic as well as a humanitarian viewpoint.

8
The Central-City Neighborhood

The preceding chapter was primarily concerned with the decline of central cities in relation to their suburbs. In reality, however, the normal daily living environment of most people is their neighborhood. (Even if workers commute to relatively distant job sites, their social life apart from that in the work place usually takes place in the neighborhood. This is especially true for persons with low or modest incomes.) To date, urban economics has contributed little to our understanding of neighborhoods, largely because they do not lend themselves to general metropolitan analyses formulated in terms of continuous mathematical functions. Also, many of the issues involved are qualitative in nature and do not lend themselves readily to quantitative analyses of particular services or programs. Nevertheless, this neglect hopefully will be corrected in the future. Although I have no pretensions in this regard, some of the issues that need to be considered are discussed in this chapter.

When people select a residence, they are likely to consider many variables. Typically, they will be interested in accessibility to major highways, the central business district, public transportation, work, shopping, schools, parks, and playgrounds. They will be interested in the characteristics of their immediate surroundings, such as street and sidewalk conditions, street lighting, street network patterns, privacy, attractiveness of the immediate environment, cleanliness, quietness, and spaciousness. They will be interested in their dwelling size and design, and the financing of its purchase or rental. They will desire adequate police and fire protection, sewage and garbage disposal facilities, water supply, and other public services. They also will be concerned about their social environment, including the socioeconomic, ethnic, and racial composition of their neighbors. These characteristics of one's residence clearly are indissociable from one's neighborhood.

Little wonder that a distinguished historian of world urban history should maintain that "limitations on size, density, and area are absolutely necessary to effective social intercourse; and they are therefore the most important instruments of rational economic and civic planning."[1] But there is little point in trying to recreate the medieval city, where the outer limits of urbanization were generally less than a half-mile from the city center. (To gain an immediate impression of the compactness of urbanization in Europe until relatively recent times, the visitor to London, Paris, Vienna, or other major European centers should set aside an afternoon to take a leisurely walk from the metropolitan center to what were the outer urban limits two or three centuries ago. One is likely to run into an expressway circling the central city but well within the outer limits of the present built-up area.)

Affinity Environment

Because people like to feel at home in the city, they tend to locate in affinity environments. An *affinity environment* has been defined as "a spatially bounded social environment that is based on voluntary residential choice and characterized by a shared preference for salient attributes such as ethnicity, life style, income, occupation, age, family status, and religion."[2]

If allowed to choose, people prefer living in social environments that are compatible with their own tastes. Give children an opportunity to design and build a model city, and they invent a city meant for children. Others prefer the bustling street life of ethnic neighborhoods. The people living in the faceless towers on Ocean Boulevard in Santa Monica are, for the most part, retired, rich, and Jewish: they came for the tranquil vistas of the Pacific Ocean. There are areas for swingers and areas for families with school-age children; there are bohemian sections and next to them marinas for yachting enthusiasts. There are districts studded with Catholic churches and others where gospel churches or synagogues predominate. There are exclusive havens for the very rich where bridle paths outnumber streets, and sections of the city where Spanish or Japanese is heard more frequently than English. The city is a system of ordered spatial diversity; its fabric is woven into a rich pattern of affinity environments.[3]

Some people want themselves and their children to be exposed to a wide variety of viewpoints, values, and types of people, rather than to be immersed in a relatively homogeneous group. This feeling is especially characteristic of many intellectuals, including those who dominate the urban-planning profession. Here are found the most ardent supporters of big-city life and the most vitriolic critics of suburbia. However, although most persons favor some exposure to a variety of viewpoints, the overwhelming majority of middle-class families choose residential locations and schools for the explicit purpose of providing value-reinforcing experiences. Thus, a study of values among urban residents showed that among all 18 subgroups analyzed, heterogeneity ranked lowest in importance, indicating that much of the planner's concern for building balanced communities and neighborhoods is not shared by the public.[4] Other studies also have suggested that the population heterogeneity advocated by many planners is unpopular with both tenants and homeowners.[5] This is no doubt "why most Jews live in predominantly Jewish neighborhoods, even in suburbs; why Catholic parents continue to support separate school systems; and partly why so few middle-class Negro families have been willing to risk moving to all-white suburbs even when there is almost no threat of any harrassment."[6]

If affinity environments resulting from voluntary residential choice were the general rule in large cities, the ghetto problem would not exist. Unfortunately, black (and some other minority) ghettos are not really affinity environments but are rather the products of racial discrimination and economic necessity. Anthony Downs has argued that:

The expansion of nonwhite residential areas has led to "massive transition" from white to nonwhite occupancy mainly because there has been no mechanism which could assure the whites in any given area that they would remain in the majority after nonwhites once began entering. Normal population turnover causes about 20 percent of the residents of the average U.S. neighborhood to move out every year because of income changes, job transfers, shifts in life-cycle position, or deaths. In order for a neighborhood to retain any given character, the persons who move in to occupy the resulting vacancies must be similar to those who have departed.

But once Negroes begin entering an all-white neighborhood near the ghetto, most other white families become convinced that the area will eventually become all Negro, mainly because this has happened so often before. Hence, it is difficult to persuade whites not now living there to move in and occupy vacancies. . . . This means that almost all vacancies are eventually occupied by nonwhites, and the neighborhood inexorably shifts toward a heavy nonwhite majority. Once this happens the remaining whites also seek to leave, since they do not wish to remain in an area where they have lost their culturally dominant position.[7]

Change in Neighborhood Composition

This process of change over a period of time in neighborhood composition has been analyzed in terms of specific dwellings, streets, and blocks.[8] It begins with initial in-movers settling in previously all-white block strips in dwelling units that are usually large and in a relatively run-down state. The initial in-movers normally purchase this housing, but if they rent, the landlord is usually an absentee owner. This stage concerns only one or two block strips and the distance between in-movers is considerable.

The second stage, that of block strip invasion, begins when whites who live near the initial in-movers leave and are replaced by blacks. At about this time, absentee owners and real estate firms purchase some of these dwellings. In this stage, the process of whites selling to blacks starts slowly but gains momentum as more and more whites leave the area.

The filling-in stage is reached when the gaps between black-occupied housing begin to close. This stage is reached sooner on streets that are openly exposed to blacks than on less exposed streets, which are more cohesive and resistant to invasion. Absentee ownership increases, the invasion process accelerates, and when filling-in has isolated pockets of whites, the consolidation stage is reached.

Throughout the process, block strips where blacks are less visible to white owners tend to be more resistant to integration. Moreover, out-movers rather than in-movers determine the overall patterns of change. It also is noteworthy that areas populated by a single ethnic group show the strongest resistance to black in-movers. A case study found that only after an "almost exclusively German neighborhood underwent an influx of Italians and other white ethnic groups did it begin to experience the arrival of blacks. It tentatively appears that the more heterogeneous an area in terms of a wide variety of social characteristics, the less resistant it is to racial invasion and succession."[9]

Breakdown of Community Structure

One of the most unfortunate aspects of the ghetto is that, unlike in the case in the voluntary affinity environments of ethnic and other groups, there tends to be a break down of community structure. David Harvey points out that reciprocity has been submerged as a mode of economic integration in the urban economy. Although reciprocity in and by itself cannot support urbanism as a way of life, it can under the right circumstances contribute greatly to the quality of urban life. "The undeniable breakdown of community structure in large cities has led to reciprocity playing a weaker and weaker role for maintaining social and economic integration."[10] James Q. Wilson maintains that the perceived breakdown of community in the case of blacks is largely a result of residential segregation and other factors that have created a condition in which there is little spatial differentiation among blacks of various class levels. The constricted supply of low-cost housing means that when middle-class blacks move into previously all-white neighborhoods, the successful incursion frequently is followed by lower-class blacks. Unless middle-class blacks can leapfrog to more distant white communities or to new communities of their own, they will be caught up in a struggle to gain hegemony over a neighborhood threatened by other blacks with quite different life-styles. In this view, the real price of segregation is not that it forces blacks and whites apart, but that it forces blacks of different classes together.[11]

Most studies of the nature of people's satisfactions and dissatisfactions with their neighborhood have had a pronounced middle-class bias and have neglected the strong concern with crime and danger that are a part of the daily life of many ghetto residents. However, one recent study that focused on crime and danger as possible determinants of dissatisfaction and of desired and actual residential mobility found that perception of crime and violence as serious neighborhood problems is strongly related to dissatisfaction with the neighborhood and to the desire to move out. Yet, subsequent actual movement to another neighborhood was practically unrelated to perception of crime and violence as serious problems.[12] In other words, most of those who wished to move out were not able to do so. An even more recent study in Detroit ranked census tract areas according to a total ecological stress index, which included measures of the socioeconomic level of census tracts as well as their degree of "instability-disorganization." One high-stress and one low-stress tract were selected from among both black and white neighborhoods. High-stress respondents had more negative perceptions and evaluations of their neighborhood than did low-stress respondents. This effect was especially strong for blacks. Dislike of neighborhood was more closely related to perceptions of its safety than to evaluations of public facilities in the area. Dislike of neighborhood also was a more important determinant of the wish to move than was dissatisfaction with respondents' housing. Although there were no follow-up data on actual mobility, responses to the question, "If you wanted to move out to a neighborhood you liked, how much *actual* chance would there be for you to move there in the next year or two?" indicated almost no correlation between the desire to move and a belief that the chances for doing so were fairly high. Thus, while respondents in high-stress areas see the neighborhood as unsafe and want to get out, they do not think the prospects for moving are very good.[13]

Abandonment

Although many ghetto residents feel trapped in their neighborhoods, in city after city there has, in fact, been a remarkable amount of ghetto housing abandonment. Crime and vandalism have played a large part in causing owners of rental housing simply to walk away from their properties, usually after allowing them to become uninhabitable by failing to maintain them and failing to pay taxes and mortgage charges.

If an apartment in a building in a high-crime neighborhood falls vacant, it is often immediately vandalized. Damage to the structure and fear of crime cause other tenants to move out. Vacancies increase. Further vandalism follows, soon leaving the building uninhabitable. When finally "abandoned," it frequently becomes a home for criminal intruders and a scene of fires, thus further contaminating the neighborhood for those living in buildings that have not yet reached that extreme state. Clearly, abandonment contributes to, and is itself a function of, neighborhood decline.[14]

In this context, an analysis of intraurban-population mobility concludes that "Brownsville, New York is a ghost town, and it is estimated that 25% of the structures in the central city of St. Louis will be abandoned within five years. Instead of experiencing high turnover rates, these areas are experiencing high rates of net outmovement, with the majority of owners relocating in adjacent areas where the cycle begins afresh. If this trend continues unchecked (and much research needs to be done if appropriate action to stop this trend is to be identified) then the residential structure of our major cities will change more rapidly in the next decade than at any other time in their past."[15]

The abandonment process can be variously interpreted. An optimistic view would be that it merely represents a normal aspect of the filter-down theory of the housing market. In New York City, for example, a considerable amount of high-rent construction took place during the 1960s but the total population remained about the same. It is possible, therefore, that the poorest tenants moved up a notch on the rent scale and vacated the worst housing units. A similar interpretation is possible in the absence of new construction if there is population decline, as in St. Louis, Cleveland, and Detroit. In this version, middle- and upper-income families leave the central city, setting in motion a series of upgrading moves by tenants. Again, the worst housing eventually is vacated and withdrawn from the market.[16]

Unfortunately, the optimistic view of the filtering process —whether initiated by new construction or population migration —neglects the fact that it is not only bad housing that is involved when abandonment sweeps a neighborhood. For example, of the 512 abandoned buildings demolished in Brooklyn in 1967, only 41 per cent were classified as substandard in the 1960 Census of Housing. A study of New York City housing also indicated that at least 80 per cent of the large "unrecorded losses" in the housing inventory from 1965 to 1967 were in buildings that had not been classified as dilapidated in a 1965 survey.[17] The picture here is not one of orderly transition but rather one of a complete breakdown of the institutional structure of the housing and property markets in low-income neighborhoods. Some housing analysts claim that abandonment is a contagious, self-fulfilling prophecy; they argue that if all owners would agree not to abandon, it is possible that none would be forced to do so or choose to do so. However, this position overlooks the two most frequently cited causes of abandonment: inadequate rent-paying capacity and high rates of neighborhood crime and violence. It is unlikely that any agreement on the part of owners to stand fast would hold up in neighborhoods where these forces are at their worst.[18]

Noncommunal Residents

Central-city blacks are not the only group of persons who have disabilities in creating and maintaining a sense of neighborhood community. Another group is composed of relatively affluent whites without children. This is by no means a homogeneous group; the young "swingers" simply lack an interest in community, while the older couples whose children have left home often lack the ability to participate meaningfully in the maintenance of community. But such persons have viable alternatives, and especially a dwelling-place environment that in effect insulates them from those threats which it is the function of community to control, i.e., they have a physical substitute for community. Yet another group of noncommunal central-city residents are the poor whites, who frequently are elderly and cannot afford to leave their neighborhoods when they change character. They also cannot afford the high-rise buildings and private security guards that for wealthier groups are the functional equivalent of communal sanctions.[19] Their feeling of vulnerability to neighborhood changes is illustrated in a Boston survey that indicated that the fear of others persons' standards of conduct was highest among those respondents who were the oldest and the poorest. "Preoccupation with such issues as the major urban problem was greater among women than among men, among those over sixty-five years of age than among those under, among Catholics more than among Jews, and among those earning less than $5000 a year more than those earning higher incomes. (Incidentally, these were *not* the same persons most explicitly concerned about and hostile to Negroes—anti-Negro sentiment was more common among middle-aged married couples who had children and modestly good incomes.)"[20]

Government Programs

Problems of maintaining viable central-city neighborhoods have in many instances been exacerbated by various government programs. These programs have usually been directed toward seemingly worthy objectives, but often too little attention has been given to unintended consequences in a larger frame of reference. Urban renewal is a case in point.

The 1949 Housing Act called for "realization, as soon as feasible . . . of a decent home and suitable living environment for every American family." It provided for a federal subsidy for low-rent public housing, a program of cheaper mortgage credit, and urban renewal of gray areas. It also envisioned the construction of 800,000 public housing units in six years. The goal of urban renewal was to improve neighborhoods by changing land-use patterns. This objective also was stressed in the Model Cities Act of 1966, which called for programs to demonstrate how a blighted neighborhood could be renewed—both physically and in terms of quality of life—by concentrating federal and local efforts in a few places with a high degree of local resident control.

By 1968 it had become clear that many neighborhoods had not really benefited from urban renewal; some were, in fact, destroyed, leaving former residents with alternatives that appeared worse than their old familiar life-style and environment.

The supply of low-income housing had definitely declined everywhere under urban renewal. This explains the unpopularity of the projects among the poor. Indeed, urban renewal projects have had the tendency to force the poor into playing a game of "musical houses." The highest-density slum area is typically selected for urban renewal; the poor are "bulldozed" out of the area and spill over into surrounding territory. They are turned into a kind of urban gypsy, raise densities elsewhere, making other areas, in turn, prime targets for urban renewal. Many critics have therefore urged that more emphasis be given to rehabilitation rather than new construction. This would preserve the social ties of existing neighborhoods, as well as their architectual merits (human-size buildings rather than high-rise "concrete jails").[21]

In the light of such criticisms, the Housing and Urban Development Act of 1968 made it clear that Congress intended residents of target areas to be benficiaries rather than victims of renewal. The act called for the creation of new dwellings and stipulated that at least 20 per cent of residential construction under urban renewal should be for low-income persons, and at least 50 per cent should be for low-income or moderate-income persons. The 1968 act and a related act passed in 1970 increased relocation aid to the displaced. The latter provided rent supplements of $1,000 for four years (or a $2,000 down payment on a home) to persons displaced by urban renewal or other federal projects. Payments also were authorized for damages up to $15,000 for homeowners, plus $300 for moving expenses. The

1968 act initiated a Neighborhood Development Program to provide parks, neighborhood city halls, training centers, and playgrounds in existing neighborhoods. And the 1969 act stipulated that for every moderate-income housing unit removed, another low-income or moderate-income unit had to be built in the same area. At this writing, support in the Executive Branch for urban renewal, model cities, open space, neighborhood facilities, and similar projects appears hesitant at best. Nevertheless, many cities are deeply involved in urban renewal as downtowns struggle for a comeback.

Urban highway construction has been another force contributing to the break up of a sense of neighborhood community. A highway, and particularly a limited access expressway, is an obvious physical obstacle when located in the middle of a neighborhood. By reducing accessibility between homes and businesses, it reduces many of the social contacts that create social cohesion. Even where highways are elevated or pedestrian bridges are provided for cross-highway movement, the highway constitutes a visual and psychological barrier between the two sides. Changed traffic patterns may also turn entire streets full of neighborhood retail establishments into a depressed area. Some such streets may become feeders to the highway and experience substantial increases in traffic load. But this, too, results in adverse changes in the local character of the affected places; people stay away from the stores and cafés they formerly frequented rather than put up with the traffic, noise, and fumes. Then, too, many homes and businesses are physically destroyed by highway projects. In recent years an average of 45,000 urban residents per year have been so displaced. Most have been middle-income and low-income people, often members of social and ethnic minorities. Highway planners have not unexpectedly shown a preference for routing new facilities through old neighborhoods rather than newer ones where more affluent families are likely to live. Parks, river and lakefront areas, and historic sites have also proven attractive places for highway planners, presumably because construction in such areas minimizes residential displacement. However, this means that urban neighborhoods must trade off scarce recreational and cultural resources for higways and related structures. Resistance to highway incursions into cities has sprouted in such diverse places as Memphis, San Antonio, Cleveland, New York, Washington, D.C., and New Orleans. A number of these efforts are particularly noteworthy because they are spearheaded by unusual coalitions of well-to-do whites and aroused blacks.[22]

Local Government Assistance

Perhaps the most difficult task for citizen groups is to gain the serious attention of city governments, which, over the past several decades, have become increasingly remote from neighborhood concerns. In part this has resulted from the increasing centralization of local government. Mayors have become stronger at the expense of city councils, city-wide organizations have become stronger at the expense of neighborhood-based political groups, and new super-agencies have been created to deal with such programs as the war on poverty, urban renewal, and public welfare. Although there have been counter-tendencies to involve city hall in neighborhood concerns, "there is a limit to how effective such responses can be, because whatever the institutional structure, the issues that most concern a neighborhood are typically those about which politicians can do relatively little."[23] For one thing, mayors are reluctant to become involved in disputes among residents of a neighborhood or between residents of adjacent neighborhoods. In addition, issues involving neighborhood quality are frequently not amenable to the services and programs approach of city governments. "Officials with experience in organizing little city halls or police-community relations programs often report that a substantial portion (perhaps a majority) of the complaints they receive concern people who 'don't keep up their houses,' or who 'let their children run wild,' or who 'have noisy parties.' Sometimes the city can do something . . . but just as often the city can do little except offer its sympathy."[24]

To point out the limitations of governments in handling neighborhood disputes within the context of existing neighborhoods and institutions is not to deny that, indirectly and over the long run, governments can do more. Certainly, they should learn from past mistakes, where public programs, in fact, contributed to the break down of neighborhood community ties.

The Ghetto

Few would deny that the most stubborn problem confronting urban policy is the existence of the ghetto, or that the present situation will be significantly changed without fundamentally new initiatives. As pointed out earlier in this chapter, the real issue is not one of racial or ethnic concentration, which has often provided constructive affinity environments for many people. It might even be argued that certain public services, such as community development activity emphasizing political participation and leadership experience, might be rendered to the poor more effectively if the poor were at least somewhat concentrated. But the ghetto slum does not even correspond to this guardedly positive view. With respect to education, to take one example, it is clear that the slum is too big.

A slum that exhausts a grade school district puts the child about two grades behind by the end of the sixth grade, so that even if he transfers to a mixed junior high school he carries a handicap from which he probably will never fully recover. Now that our biggest city slums have grown to high school district size, chronic unemployment is almost ensured. A neighborhood, moreover, which breeds a conniving, mistrusting youth who seeks only the quick payoff and self-preservation will hardly prepare him to be a disciplined laboratory technician in a cooperative scientific venture, or for other "jobs with a future."[25]

Thus, contrary to the views of segregationists, black militants, and many well-meaning whites who favor refurbishing the ghetto, it would seem that any long-run solution to problems of central-city poverty will have to involve a major dispersal of its low-income population. John Kain and Joseph Persky have argued in no uncertain terms that:

nothing less than a complete change in the structure of the metropolis . . . will solve the problems of the ghetto. Indeed, it is ironic, almost cynical, the extent to which current programs that ostensibly are concerned with the welfare of urban Negroes are willing to accept and are even based upon the permanence of central ghettos. Thus, under every heading of social welfare legislation, education, income transfer, employment, and housing we find programs that can only serve to strengthen the ghetto and the serious problems that it generates. In particular, these programs concentrate on beautifying the fundamentally ugly structure of the current metropolis and not on providing individuals with the tools necessary to break out of the structure. The shame of the situation is that viable alternatives do exist.[26]

These alternatives include improved information made available to black job-seekers, strong job-training programs linked to employment opportunities in industry, and improved transportation between black residential areas and suburban employment sites. Instead of urban renewal and public-housing projects that reinforce racial and economic separation, the supply of low-income housing outside the ghetto should be greatly expanded. Rent subsidies and vigorous enforcement of open-housing laws would give developers, lenders, and realtors an excuse to act in their own economic self-interest. Even if residential segregation is maintained, or if blacks prefer to live among other blacks, there can be suburbanization of blacks without housing integration. The creation of a number of dispersed black communities would place blacks closer to suburban job opportunities and, by reducing pressures on central neighborhood housing markets, improve the chances for private renewal of middle-income neighborhoods.[27]

It would only be realistic to expect that massive ghetto dispersal would be resisted by suburban whites and even by some blacks, who might prefer living with other blacks in a highly urbanized environment. Why then even consider such a strategy? Because preserving the ghetto's lack of employment possibilities, poor educational opportunities, poverty, and violence seems an even more undesirable alternative. Moreover, the persistence of the ghetto may well make the goal of equal opportunity even more difficult to achieve in the future.

In weighing the advantages and disadvantages of ghetto dispersal, as well as the forms dispersal might take, certain basic principles should be kept in mind.[28] First, any dispersal program will have to involve significant participation by the private sector, or else there is too great a risk that ghetto blacks (like many Appalachian whites) will become too dependent on the government. Second, any actions undertaken should be linked to incentives that will appeal to the self-interest of all groups concerned and to their consciences. For example, business loses potential profits and output because poor blacks lack the means to engage in high-level consumption, and black workers' lack of education and training makes them unable to compete for better-paying jobs. Third, a dispersal program must involve a high degree of participation by blacks. Lack of skill and experience may mean that initially the exercise of power and authority will be disorderly, inefficient, and even corrupt. But this was also the case among other minorities. A significant degree of self-determination is a necessary prelude to equality. Finally, no solution to ghetto problems is possible unless it is supported by a majority of the white middle class. "This group," as Anthony Downs maintains, "must be persuaded to expend many resources, and alter its own traditional behavior, in order to produce outcomes that appear to benefit mainly a small minority of the population. Moreover, parts of that minority are likely to become dissatisfied and vocally discontent the more benefits the minority achieves. This makes the persuasion problem doubly difficult."[29]

Summary

The present chapter began by emphasizing that the neighborhood—a neglected phenomenon in the economics literature—is the context in which most people seek a sense of community. It is this sense of community that helps support and give meaning to one's own individuality. While many persons have the good fortune to live in affinity environments, many others do not. Particular attention has been given here to the break down of the neighborhood in the central cities of large metropolitan areas, a phenomenon that has affected diverse groups of people but especially black ghetto residents. It has been argued that solutions to this problem will require fundamental changes in the spatial form of metropolitan areas.

Some critics have abandoned all hope of making central cities viable living places in the foreseeable future. While this despair may be premature, the evidence indicates that a genuine effort to disperse ghetto residents (perhaps to smaller but still clustered areas of the suburbs), or at least a substantial number of them, must be made if they and their children and grandchildren are to participate in the opportunities that this nation is supposedly committed to extending to all of its citizens. Such an effort will have to receive the support of a majority of the white middle class now entrenched in the suburbs. But while we ask that they explicitly and constructively bring the poor and blacks into planning for metropolitan growth and development, it also is apparent that they have problems of their own related to the spatial organization of metropolitan areas.

9

The Growth Controversy in the Suburbs

The postwar rush to the suburbs was occasioned by the conjunction of a number of factors, including a desire for quasicountry living, a baby boom that increased demand for residential space, a high degree of mobility made possible by mass ownership of automobiles, high and rising incomes, and federal policies that made it relatively easy to finance suburban housing. As suburban communities sprang up, they were determined to preserve what they considered to be their own territory and way of life. Zoning was widely adopted and often used as a device to maintain relatively homogeneous affinity environments. With the cooperation of the courts, vast tracts of land were given over to housing and other infrastructure that virtually guaranteed the same class of residents. For the white and the nonpoor, at least, the classic American pattern of upward mobility posed no problem. As a family made more money, it simply traded in its old house and acquired a new one in a more affluent development. Thus, was the "good life" pursued.

For many of the speculative developers of the suburbs, it was indeed a good life. Their highly profitable ventures were often a consequence of cheap land, failure to provide public amenities beyond streets and utilities, and quick and shoddy construction. But they also benefited from the tacit complicity of the suburbanites, who were preoccupied with house and lawn, willing to forego community life and public amenities, and willing to tolerate wide spatial separation of work from residence.

Suburban Growth

Although Americans have become increasingly suburbanized in the past three decades, a growing number of citizens are conscious that new development may involve economic hardships as well as harmful environmental effects. There seems to be more awareness of —and less willingness to tolerate—traffic congestion that impedes

Table 9-1
Areas with Growth Constraints, March 1973

STATES

Delaware	Selected growth
Hawaii	Control growth
New Hampshire	Selective growth
Oregon	Selective growth
Vermont	Selective growth

POSSIBLE CANDIDATES

Maine	Selective growth
Colorado	Selective growth

COUNTIES, CITIES, AND TOWNSHIPS

Brentwood, Calif.	Limit growth
Fremont, Calif.	Slow growth
Jenner, Calif.	Slow growth
Livermore, Calif.	Limit growth
Milpitas, Calif.	Slow growth
Palm Springs, Calif.	Control growth
Palo Alto, Calif.	Slow growth
Petaluma, Calif.	Slow, control growth
Pleasanton, Calif.	Limit growth
Sacramento County, Calif.	Control, limit growth
Santa Clara County, Calif.	Slow growth
San Diego, Calif.	Control growth
San Francisco ABAG, Calif.	Slow growth
San Jose, Calif.	Slow, control growth
Ventura, Calif.	Slow growth
Boulder, Colo.	Slow, control, limit growth
Colorado Springs, Colo.	Slow, control growth
West Windsor, Conn.	Slow growth
Boca Raton, Fla.	Limit growth
Palm Beach County, Fla.	Slow growth
Sarasota County, Fla.	Slow growth
Boise, Ida.	Control growth
Amherst, Mass.	Slow growth
Lincoln, Mass.	Slow growth
Minneapolis-St. Paul Metro Council, Minn.	Limit growth
Lincoln, Neb.	Control growth
Portsmouth, N.H.	Slow growth
Madison, Twp, N.J.	Slow, limit growth
Mahwah, N.J.	Slow growth
No. Bergen Twp., N.J.	Slow growth
Ramapo, N.Y.	Slow, control growth
Rockland County, N.Y.	Slow growth
Astoria, Ore.	Slow growth
Eugene, Ore.	Slow growth
Salem, Ore.	Slow growth

Table 9-1 (Continued)

Arlington County, Va.	Slow, control, limit growth
Charlottesville, Va.	Control growth
Fairfax County, Va.	Slow growth
Loudon County, Va.	Slow, control growth

POSSIBLE CANDIDATES

Tuscon, Ariz.	Slow growth
Los Angeles County, Calif.	Slow, limit growth
Orange County, Calif.	Control, limit growth
Dade County, Fla.	Control growth
Ann Arbor, Mich.	Slow growth
Warwick, R.I.	Slow, limit growth
Cranston, R.I.	Slow, limit growth

Source: Earl Finkler, "Nongrowth: A Review of the Literature," American Society of Planning Officials Planning Advisory Service Report No. 289 (March 1973), p. 18, from information supplied by the Urban Land Institute.

commuting, inappropriate buildings that clutter former open spaces and scenic landmarks, and signs of air, water, noise, and solid-waste pollution, especially when it intrudes at close proximity. In presenting their cases, developers have attempted to demonstrate that their projects will increase the tax base, create more trade for local business, stimulate new employment opportunities, and generally improve the economy of the community. What they neglect to discuss are the full costs of these projects. What will growth do to the community's school system, public services, public utilities, transportation, and recreation facilities? What will it cost to meet the new demands resulting from growth? Most city and county officials have been too busy working out their day-to-day problems to have time to come to grips adequately with such questions. Nevertheless, they are less willing than formerly to assume that new growth automatically brings new jobs and more tax benefits, reflecting the personal experience of many taxpayers that the full costs required to accommodate growth can be more than the benefits. Indeed, a large and growing number of places now have, or are seriously considering, legal constraints on future growth (see Table 9-1).

The issue of rapid suburban growth arises even in metropolitan areas that are growing around the national average rate, which was 16.6 per cent between 1960 and 1970. With central-city population declines of 10 to 20 percent over a decade, the suburban growth rate can be leveraged to 100 to 200 per cent. Moreover, in recent years there has been a pronounced tendency for developers to leapfrog over expensive land close to metropolitan areas to find cheaper sites farther out. Less expensive distant houses lure residents and businesses from the central cities, reducing their tax bases. Mass transportation is not economical in the far suburbs, so their residents become totally dependent on the auto, increasing the strain on the nation's scarce fuel supplies. Moreover, more than 10,000 governmental units now provide transportation, water, waste disposal, and other public services in an essentially haphazard fashion.

When state land regulation comes up, city and county officials and their organizations typically respond by opposing any relinquishment of authority, however unwilling or incapable they have been to exercise it. At present, state land-use policies are little more than an aggregate of thousands of unrelated and often conflicting decisions made by single purpose agencies, local and regional governments, and private developers. No state has a working mechanism for dealing with the totality of its land. Even Hawaii, in spite of having broadly zoned all its land over a decade ago, has continual controversies over activities within zones, and pressures are being exerted to create a new administrative mechanism.

Effect of Tax Policies

At the federal level, tax policies have had a clear and strong effect in encouraging speculation and low-density suburban sprawl. An analysis of San Jose, California and its metropolitan area, Santa Clara county, found that:

Theoretically, City and County authorities could have resisted the pressures to annex, to rezone, and to do all the other things that permitted the sprawl. Politically, however, the speculative pressures were so great as to be virtually uncontrollable. And a major reason for such pressures has been the incentive to real estate speculation coming from the break given to such speculation on the Federal income tax. We have estimated, for example, that the money flowing to Santa Clara County in one year from just one of a number of tax advantages—capital gains treatment of speculative gains—is greater than the total expenditure in the County of the Department of Housing and Urban Development in the same year.[1]

Because of capital-gains tax advantages, the large corporate or individual speculator has his tax liability on increases in the value of land and buildings reduced from the 50 per cent (or possibly more in the case of the individual) it would be taxed as straight income, to a maximum of 25 per cent. In addition, there are several ways in which even the capital-gains tax can be postponed as the real estate investor's equity increases. For example, a piece of property can be exchanged for a larger piece of property with no current tax; and this process can be repeated through a series of successive exchanges. Property also can be refinanced so as to withdraw cash without tax. If property is involuntarily converted for public use, the gains from the condemnation proceeding can be reinvested; this also holds for insurance proceeds in the event of casualty loss. If property is held through the owner's lifetime, the unrealized appreciation may be capitalized through the tax-free step-up of basis to fair market value at the time of the owner's death. The effect of this revaluation may restore all the depreciation that the owner may have deducted during his lifetime. Postponement until death applies only to individuals and not to corporations, but it can be used with both land speculation and new building. In addition, the high-income taxpayer, including the corporation, can deduct the current costs of maintaining the property, including local property taxes, at very little cost to himself because of his high tax bracket. Finally, the builder in particular can obtain substantial savings by depreciating his structures down to zero tax value at an accelerated rate (if he holds and rents his buildings) and then by selling them at their true value, which is much more than zero. While this provision is most important in its effects on slum property turned over from owner to owner, with each owner establishing a new tax basis at his purchase price, the overall effect of the federal income tax structure has been to encourage low-density rather than high-density residential development. However, the structure has considerable potential for promoting high-density development through cooperative apartment construction.[2]

Zoning Laws

Land-use regulation in the United States has traditionally been a constitutional power delegated by the states to counties and cities. Their principal implement has been zoning. Over the years, most metropolitan municipalities have enacted zoning ordinances that limit the nature of land use in various parts of their jurisdictions. Although originally devised to promote rational land-use planning, they have been increasingly criticized for their baneful effects on the metropolitan system.

Zoning laws have been used to restrict land use in the belief that this will provide more open space and green and wooded areas. Environmentalists have tended to look with favor at measures that would leave more of nature as it is, undisturbed by development and people. However, as so often happens, the unintended or ignored consequences of a policy may have a result different from, or even the opposite of, the intended goal. In the present case, the aim of land conservation can operate to waste it. Two kinds of zoning may have this effect. First are those regulations that reduce density by limiting the amount of dwelling units on an acre of land. Second are those that prohibit high-rise or low-rise multiple-family construction. To require one house on two acres of land when a family would be quite satisfied with less space amounts to a waste of land and the homeowner's money. Limitations or prohibitions against apartments, condominiums, and townhouses are likewise wasteful. Each floor of a multilevel building such as an apartment in effect adds to the supply of land.

Zoning ordinances can also be used to preserve and enhance the tax base of a community, though only industrial and commercial activities of the "right sort" are encouraged. At the same time, zoning to preserve the quality of the community serves to keep out low-income, welfare, and minority groups. (Although courts have overturned zoning that discriminates racially, they have been more lenient with respect to zoning that discriminates economically. In recent years civil rights groups have sought to challenge the constitutionality of suburban zoning, but it is generally difficult to prove that particular cases of zoning are discriminatory and in violation of civil rights.) The encouragement of (some) economic activity combined with the exclusion of workers has created problems in suburban areas. For example, a 20 per cent annual turnover rate of production workers at a Ford assembly plant in northern New Jersey has been attributed to a shortage of nearby housing for workers. Twenty local governments in the Princeton area have zoned enough undeveloped land for industrial parks and research centers to support 1.2 million jobs. Yet, the undeveloped residential land in the area is zoned for such low densities that it could house only 144,000 workers.[3] The other side of the suburban exclusion coin is the concentration of poor and minorities in central-city neighborhoods, an issue considered in detail in Chapter 8.

To counter those who argue that the abandonment of zoning would bring about chaos and instability in real estate markets, the case of Houston frequently is cited. The nation's sixth largest city has no zoning; yet, real estate is no less stable or valuable than in other major cities. Some Houstonians live on large sites and others on small ones, depending on income and preferences. Overall, there seems to be no more proliferation of different land uses than elsewhere; residential areas are as devoid of factories and quick-service prepared food outlets as in places with zoning. It is argued that Houston's lack of zoning also has positive advantages. It facilitates planning—albeit by private developers—because it makes it easier to put together large tracts of land for major development projects; defenders of Houston's attitude toward zoning maintain that, relative to other cities, this phenomenon benefits the central city even more than the suburbs. Another advantage is a minimum of political control over land use; city council members cannot change restrictions for the benefit of those with political influence. Of course, lack of zoning is not equivalent to absolute laissez-faire. Houston has a number of specified land-use ordinances regulating the minimum lot size for a single-family dwelling, street setbacks, off-street parking, slaughterhouse locations, density of mobile homes, and some other land uses. Restrictive covenants—private legal agreements that generally prohibit multifamily, commercial, and industrial uses within single-family subdivisions—also play an important role and are enforced by the city.

Whatever one's view concerning the zoning issue, it is by no means the only way in which local growth may be restricted or slowed. Fort Lauderdale's publicity and advertising department was publicly funded for two decades and had a 1972 budget of $580,000. It was recently closed. The state of Oregon has let it be known that in-migration is no longer wanted (especially by Californians?). During a recent visit to New Mexico I passed a large billboard in Sandoval County that carried a very simple and direct message: "Undevelop New Mexico." The self-proclaimed sponsor was a group calling itself the New Mexico Undevelopment Commission. (Unfortunately, the billboard partially blocked a magnificent panoramic view of the desert and mountains.) In spite of such efforts, negative advertising still has the effect of drawing attention to the places in question, and the implicit message is that the people who live in them regard them as very attractive. One may even speculate that negative advertising is more positively persuasive than run-of-the-mill boosterism; when people have something to hide (legally), it must be good.

Community Programs

For suburban communities the Ramapo Plan is a potentially more effective means for limiting growth. Ramapo is a prosperous community in Rockland County, N.Y., about 35 miles from New York City; between 1960 and 1970 it doubled in population. Local citizens feared that leaving growth to the developers would have detrimental environmental consequences, meaning in part that the integrity of the rolling landscape would be threatened by a sea of small houses. The first step in response was to draw up a master plan for the area and then a zoning ordinance based on that plan. In anticipation of future development, the township established a long-term capital-improvements program. By 1969 the package of coordinated controls was in effect. Now, before any project is approved it must be shown that it conforms to the master plan and will not overload municipal services, including sewers, drainage, parks and recreation areas, roads, and firehouses. If these services do not yet exist, the developer must wait until the township builds them on schedule or else he must install them at his own cost. In 1972 landowners and developers brought suit to overthrow the program. But the New York State Court of Appeals upheld—and even praised—the Ramapo Plan.

Boca Raton, Florida, north of Miami, is another community whose resistance to unbridled growth has received wide publicity. In the face of a 600 per cent growth rate in the past dozen years, Boca Raton, which now has about 50,000 residents, amended the city charter to allow no more than 40,000 dwelling units, including individual houses, apartments, and condominiums. With an average of

2.5 persons per units, this would mean that after a population of 100,000 is reached no more building permits would ever be granted.

Boulder, Colorado has been described as the city with the greatest "public consciousness that growth can be controlled or significantly affected as a matter of public policy."[4] Between 1960 and 1970, Boulder's population grew from 37,000 to 67,000. In November 1971 the municipal election ballot contained a resolution that sought to place a 100,000 limit on the city's population. Although it was defeated by about a three-to-two ratio, a companion resolution was approved by over 70 per cent of the voters. It stated that: "The city government, working with the county government, shall take all steps necessary to hold the rate of growth in the Boulder Valley to a level substantially below that experienced in the 1960s and shall insure that the growth that does take place shall provide living qualities in keeping with the policies found in the Boulder Valley Comprehensive Plan."[5] The plan covers about 58 square miles in and around Boulder; when it was published in 1970 it anticipated that the population in the valley would double in the next two decades. Noting that Boulder's pursuit of no growth (or more accurately limited growth) is like having four aces and trying to lose, Wilbur Thompson remarks that:

local land values and house prices would rise sharply if the growth pressures were restrained for very long. Presumably nothing has changed the attractiveness of Boulder as a place to live. In fact, to the high bidders—the educated and the affluent of the Denver area—this already favored place, now protected from invading hordes, could easily be even more attractive than before. All in all, it is hard to avoid concluding that this, for some, primrose path avoids the pitfalls of growth by driving the poor out of town. This may not have been the proponents' intention but "the road to hell." And the "poor" could come to include college instructors with families bigger than their incomes.[6]

In support of Thompson's argument it may be noted that in Boca Raton, a moratorium was placed on all building permits to prevent a chaotic construction binge in the wake of the city's decision to impose a population limit. As a result, the price of vacant land rose by more than 25 per cent in a few months, and the value of existing homes increased by at least 15 per cent.[7] In an article on Boca Raton, the *New York Times* asked: "Do homeowners have the right to impose their will on the property rights of the real estate developer and speculator, beyond the nominal circumstances of zoning and building controls? And does the community have the right to shut out the rest of the world like a medieval wall city?"[8] At this writing, a California court decision has given an answer.

Petaluma, a community of 30,000 persons north of San Francisco, doubled in population in the past decade. In 1972 it passed a law limiting housing growth to 2,500 units between then and 1977. A suit contesting the legality of Petaluma's ordinance was initiated by two builders' associations—a land company and a local property owner. They contended that if the entire San Francisco Bay region adopted similar laws there would be a decline in housing quality and a shortage of some 105,000 housing units within six years. The federal judge who ruled in the case maintained that Petaluma's restriction interfered with the constitutional "right to travel" of people who might want to move there. While expressing sympathy with the cause of orderly growth, he held that if many communities or states set population limits and closed their borders, the effect would be to immobilize the population. According to the ruling, no local government has an inherent right to limit growth merely to maintain a certain kind of environment. In response, the mayor of Petaluma stated that the city was trying to plan for growth rather than put a sudden stop to it. Clearly, the rulings of appellate courts will be of crucial significance for communities that have, or intend to, place limitations on their future growth.

Marin County, like Petaluma, is north of San Francisco. It has tried to discourage growth by limiting public services, e.g., a water bond issue recently was voted down for this reason. Indeed, the entire San Francisco Bay area illustrates the polarity between no-growth sentiment in the suburbs and the needs of people in the central city. The area has four of the nation's top 28 counties in terms of median family income: Marin ($13,935), San Mateo ($13,222), Santa Clara ($12,456), and Contra Costa ($12,423). Yet, at the time of the 1970 census, over 150,000 families were living below the poverty threshhold; just over a quarter lived in San Francisco and another 14 per cent in Oakland.

The case for no growth in the affluent suburbs "is bound to be highly suspect when the protectors live sprawled over half- and full-acre lots, with two or more cars in every driveway, and when they make waste in the good old American way. Any policy which permits the local inhabitants to hold their numbers in check simply so they can push their consumption per capita to the limit would seem to be more self-indulgent than environment-concerned."[9] Even without questioning the motives of the suburban no-growth advocates, it could still be argued that they should be willing to give up something in order to have the environmental quality and population stability they desire. They should be willing to make trade-offs so that their restrictions at least are not regressive.

Protection of the environment has come to be seen as primarily a suburban concern. But the issue should be at least as important to the central cities, where air pollution and congestion affect daily living more than suburbanities are affected by new development. Also, because the central-city poor are less mobile, they are less able to escape environmental disamenities. Thus, efforts similar to those now devoted to saving suburban open space should be directed toward cleaning up the central city. Economic growth not desired by the suburbs could also be directed to central cities. Moreover, when suburban growth restrictions result in higher land prices that keep people out, the trade-off for such exclusiveness might be the willingness to reimburse the central city for housing the poor. One way of making the trade-off explicit would be for the state to require that public housing referendums, which usually fail, be attached to open-space referendums, which usually pass. The suburbs voting for open space but not for public housing would be required by the state to transmit funds representing the public cost of such units to cities that would be willing to provide housing for low-income families. Similarly, builders could be required to include housing for low-income people in each subdivision or else contribute toward a city fund to purchase low-income housing sites. Covenants requiring that a certain number of units be sold or rented to families with incomes under a certain level, and density bonuses stipulating that builders provide low-income housing quotas, are among the devices that could be used, at least experimentally, to increase the amount of suburban housing available to the poor.[10]

Petaluma restricted 10 per cent of its annual building permit quota for low- and moderate-cost housing. However, the difficulty with this ordinance, and that in Ramapo, is that there is no guarantee that builders will actually construct the low-income units. If the latter are to be supplied, they probably should be allocated for simultaneous use with others in the quota. Such an incentive might force the builder to find ways of making housing available to the poor at a profit, even if more expensive houses subsidize the less expensive.

Fairfax County, Virginia, a rapidly growing suburb of Washington, D.C., has passed an ordinance to make all developments of more than fifty dwellings include housing for low- and moderate-income groups. At this writing it is being contested in the courts. Fairfax also requires that developers describe the environmental impact of their projects before construction is approved; and some $2 million from revenue-sharing funds will be budgeted for buying unspoiled property for land banks. Next on the agenda is a study of whether the county can recapture through a rezoning tax some of the increased land value created by public outlays for new roads, schools, and sewers. Fairfax's attempts to orchestrate rather than stop growth and its willingness to deal forthrightly with difficult social issues place it clearly in the vanguard of creative suburban communities.

Federal and State Policies

Perhaps other suburban communities would be more innovative if pressures at the federal level and constraints imposed at the state level were modified. After all, it simply is not true that all local public officials are foolish if not corrupt, or that all planners are hesitant and ineffectual. It would appear desirable for the federal government to change some policies that directly or indirectly distort the form and growth of metropolitan areas. Reforms in the tax policy already discussed would be desirable. National military procurement policies and major federal facility locations have been major sources of growth in many parts of the country, but little systematic planning has been done in this regard. More vigorous efforts to eliminate housing discrimination, no matter under what pretense it is being maintained, combined with federal assumption of welfare costs and income maintenance, would promote more freedom of choice and better housing opportunities for low- and middle-income families.

State policies also need to be altered. For example, state assumption of educational costs would create more equal opportunity and lift yet another burden from property and housing, especially if it were accompanied by a shift from property tax to income tax for revenue. Ground rules set at the state level have permitted extreme diffusion of powers and functional responsibilities among local government. Within the narrow constraints imposed by state legislatures, municipalities have little incentive to adopt a regional or even county-wide perspective.

In view of the complexity of the problems confronting metropolitan areas, it is not to be expected that even well-meaning reforms will automatically provide easy solutions. For example, removal of exclusionary zoning—for which liberals have long fought—could accentuate racial segregation. It might be that the suburban housing thus made available would be snapped up by whites who heretofore have not been willing or able to leave the central cities. Building code enforcement, another seemingly positive measure, could lead to higher rents for poor people or even to demolition, leaving the poor family with no dwelling at all.

On the other hand, the courts might be persuaded to respond favorably to no-growth and restricted-growth suburban policies if they were based less on self-indulgence and more on a considered, balanced approach to such things as transportation, employment, housing, schools, and the quality of life. In this vein, Thompson suggests that a sympathetic hearing might be given a community whose policy was

(a) founded on strong land use controls that looked with special favor on multiple dwellings and/or cluster development; (b) synchronized with a public transportation plan that reinforced low fare (or no fare) transit with selective automobile tolls and prohibitions; (c) designed to bring home and work to within walking or bicycling distance in many circumstances; and (d) was, of course, financed so as to make ample provision for subsidized low income housing. A serious agenda of good faith should precede the exercise of the power to deny admission to town, that is, to restrict the rights of others.[11]

Planning and Cooperation

Finally, the interconnected interests of communities within metropolitan areas would suggest that there should be instutional vehicles for cooperation. But cooperative efforts are not easily organized. How is agreement to be obtained on such issues as the voting rules to be used and the criteria for designating boundaries? Moreover, urban policymaking is essentially a socio-political process; resolution of conflict among groups with divergent interests is very rarely a matter of simple intellectual and deliberative choice. Conflicting views of the best form of spatial organization may arise because different facilities can best be provided at different scales. Transportation and sewage systems, for example, may be most efficiently organized on a metropolitan-wide basis, whereas day-care centers and playgrounds can best be organized at the level of the neighborhood. Even here, though, problems are likely to be present because self-interest often conflicts with the interests of the community as a whole. In such situations, "The smaller groups —the privileged and intermediate groups—can often defeat the large groups—which are normally supposed to prevail in democracy. . . . because the former are generally organized and active while the latter are normally unorganized and inactive."[12]

Some hard questions also can be asked about the planning function. How will planners be selected, and what alternatives will there be if citizens are not satisfied? Can large bureaucracies effectively plan actions in complex environments, or will their outputs be the result of many individuals interacting within their own smaller environmental constraints? Can coordination occur in nondirected ways? Is better training for planning professionals the way to solutions?[13] Whatever the answers to these questions—and they are likely to vary according to particular local circumstances—past experience does permit certain generalizations concerning institutional means for dealing with regional problems within metropolitan areas. For example, evaluations of cooperative or confederative approaches, such as councils of governments, indicate that they are seriously deficient in coping with major metropolitan problems. City-county consolidation has proven constructive, but it rarely takes in the whole of a metropolitan region. Metropolitan governments have difficulty in coping with the wide variety of requirements, preferences, and resources in the various parts of their jurisdictions. Perhaps the most effective approach would be some form of two-tier government, offering regionalism where it is needed along with local control where it is appropriate. The principal deficiency of most two-tier approaches has been their inadequacy with respect to incorporating new growth in an orderly way,[14] the issue which has been the main concern of this chapter.

Clearly, we are still a long way from organizing effectively to attain more rational suburban development and to bring about solutions for central city-suburban conflicts. Nevertheless the issues have been sharpened in recent years, and have been given wide publicity. In the immediate future, fresh initiatives from the federal government are not to be expected; the administration has made it apparent that it wants state and local problems defined and dealt with at these levels. In spite of the obvious differential spatial impact of federal programs and policies, there is little likelihood that their effects, both intended and unintended, will be systematically treated within the framework of a national urban-growth policy, even though Congress has called for such a policy. For now, the extent to which states and communities can be and will be responsive to the problems raised here represents a fundamental test of American democracy.

10 Cluster Development

A major characteristic of metropolitan growth is the presence of many separate nodes or subcenters of concentrated development. For example, wherever breaks occur along transportation routes, as in the case of railroad or rapid transit line stations, there is a tendency for businesses to cluster. Other activities may also lead to concentration in a wide variety of metropolitan locations. Industrial parks, recreation facilities, schools, universities, and shopping malls attract people and related economic activities that benefit from agglomeration economies. As new nodes become established, they become traffic generators, so that the metropolitan area gradually develops a multinuclear structure. Partial explanations can be given for the size and location of metropolitan subcenters, although a satisfactory general theory has yet to be worked out. Central-place theory provides one such explanation.

Central-Place Theory

The "range" of a good and a "threshold" population (or purchasing power size) are the key concepts in central-place theory. The *range* of a good denotes the zone around the central place from which persons travel to the center to purchase the good or service offered at the place. In theory, the upper limit of this range is the maximum possible sales radius. Beyond this limit, the price of the good is too high because the distance involved makes it so or because of the closer proximity of consumers to alternative centers. The lower limit of the range is the radius that encloses the minimum number of consumers necessary to provide a sales volume adequate for the good to be supplied profitably from the central place. This lower limit is the *threshold* population. The lowest level of center performs certain functions or provides certain goods that are limited in number and kind by the limited population within usual range of the center. The center of the next highest order performs all the functions of the lower-order center, plus a group of additional functions. The next highest order of center will offer all the goods offered by the first two levels but will be differentiated from the order just beneath by a group of goods with greater ranges than those possessed by any of the goods of the next smaller center. In this manner a hierarchy of centers is determined.

It should be pointed out that population by itself is not necessarily a good measure of centrality. A large, specialized-function center may have only a small hinterland area and little influence on it. Thus, centrality is better considered in terms of centralized services, including administration, culture, health and social services, organization of economic and social life, finance, trade, service industries, the labor market, and traffic.

Central-place theory can explain why a consumer-serving activity that can reach full economies of scale and agglomeration without having to serve the entire metropolitan area from one place will increase its proximity to consumers by moving to shopping centers, each of which serves only a part of the entire metropolitan area. Each shopping center represents in turn a concentration of employment and a focus for access for work, shopping, and recreational trips. However, central-place theory does not explain why some subcenters are functionally differentiated in some ways that have nothing to do with their relative size or their level in the central place hierarchy. Subcenters do not merely duplicate the central business district; there are some activities that concentrate at one place within the metropolitan area but away from the center because the latter is not an economic location. Such activities typically do not use land intensively enough to afford downtown sites, yet, their internal access needs require a more compact area than would be obtained from a ring pattern of location. For example, a university campus might best be located five miles from the center of the metropolitan area that supplies most of its students. A more central location would mean excessive land costs, whereas a peripheral location would mean poor commuting access for most students, and perhaps too great a distance from desirable urban activities. If one were to apply a location model based on concentric ring patterns around the metropolitan center, a 300-acre campus located five miles from the center would be about 80 feet wide and more than 31 miles long.

Since such a layout would preclude both having a sizable stadium and getting to classes on time, it is clearly unacceptable. In the interests of its own internal logistics, the university would prefer a blob to a doughnut. Two different institutions in the same city might find some external-economy advantage in being close to one another in a single "university district," but if they are intensely competing for commuter students, they might prefer to locate on opposite sides of town.

The point here is that a university is a locational unit subject to considerable *economies of scale*, so that there will be only a few unit locations, perhaps only one, in any given urban area; while at the same time it is sufficiently space using to need an off-center or even suburban location. The same principle applies to any activity with these characteristics.[1]

Other examples of this phenomenon would thus include research centers, cultural centers, concentrations of auto sales lots, and, increasingly, wholesale produce markets and other wholesaling activities. On the other hand, the construction of beltways around some metropolitan areas has made it feasible for some activities to locate along a significant part of the arc, or doughnut. The location of electronics and other light—though often technologically sophisticated—industries along Highway 128 in the Boston area is a classic example.

The growth of concentrated subcenters may have still other causes. Firms which export their products may prefer sites that maximize accessibility by locating near the junctions of major highways; others may prefer to be close to a major airport. Especially in instances where the topography is rough, activities may cluster on the relatively flat sites available, even if they do not have the best access. Yet another kind of tendency to concentration is found in certain types of residential land use; preferences for affinity environments, discussed in the previous two chapters, act as an agglomerative force for particular classes of residence, even where low densities are involved. Moreover, if better educated, higher income groups concentrate in a given subcenter or set of subcenters on one side of the metropolitan area, trade and service activities aimed particularly at these groups will have their point of maximum market access potential somewhere at the same end of the metropolitan area.

Urban Structure

The increasing metropolitanization of the American population, the flexibility of the auto and truck, and the increased range of access made possible by the construction of the Interstate Highway System and other major highway networks, have caused many metropolitan areas to coalesce. Anticipated trends indicate a continuance of the rapid sprawl and coalescence of separate areas into metropolitan and megalopolitan complexes (see Figure 2-4, Chapter 2). To the extent that such tendencies continue, multinuclear forms will become a basic characteristic of urban structure. In 1968, 33 of the SMSAs designated by the U.S. Bureau of the Census had double names, such as Minneapolis-St. Paul, and 15 had triple names, such as Gary-Hammond-East Chicago. By 1973 these respective groups had increased to 50 and 23 SMSAs, respectively.

Is there a viable alternative to the sprawling agglomerations that characterize so many current urban growth patterns? Wilfred Owen has forcefully argued for one that appears attractive. Owen implicitly assumes that urbanization will continue and that people will be loath to give up the freedom of movement represented by the auto, no matter what the arguments of the mass transportation advocates. He also recognizes the advantages of clustered development in terms of access to opportunities. What Owen proposes is a regional city whose attributes appear to conform with the dominant location-preference patterns discussed in Chapter 3. The regional city

is made up of interconnected clusters surrounded by low-density land uses, where the special benefits of concentration can be enjoyed without succumbing to a continuous urban buildup unrelated to the countryside. The multicentered city offers a compromise between undesirably high density and the destructive side effects of indiscriminate sprawl . . . .

An interconnected system of moderate-sized communities could create a sense of belonging and provide a basis for local self-government. At the same time scale economies could be realized through regionwide provision of transit, highways, sewage treatment, waterworks, and electric power. Regional cities of the future will combine the best aspects of both concentration and dispersal . . . in a setting that permits a closer relation between man and the natural environment.[2]

Owen points out that many modern airports are good examples of development clusters with their own internal transport system as well as connections with the outside. Some have rail connections with the central city, and some have advanced systems for internal circulation, including moving belts for baggage and freight, moving walkways for passengers, and a variety of clustered services such as hotels, restaurants, meeting rooms, theaters, and art exhibits. Houston's Intercontinental airport is programmed to grow by duplicating units that are considered to be optimal, rather than allowing increased activity to interfere with clusters that already are performing well. "The total system suggests the physical layout of a regional city comprising pedestrian clusters connected by major transport routes."[3]

But the analogy can be pushed too far. Owen regards with favor the minisubway system connecting Houston Intercontinental terminals, but also notes that it is possible to walk through the tunnel. The new Dallas-Ft. Worth Airport has pushed the cellular growth concept even further than Houston Intercontinental, but does not allow for walking from one terminal to another. Thus, even if one could easily walk to a connecting flight (the airport is a major center for feeder flights that connect with long distance runs) at the terminal on the left, it is necessary to take a small train or bus that goes to the right and has to make nearly a complete circuit before arriving at the intended terminal. If at the end of this unnecessary journey one finds that his plane has just pulled away from the gate, he may well reflect on the mixed blessings of modern technology.

Moreover, whatever the attractiveness of even the most diverse of airport development clusters, few people seem to have any desire to linger over their amenities. Persons in transit nearly always want to minimize the time spent in any airport, and visitors still come more to watch the planes than to be entertained by the airport per se. Large shopping malls have also been highly touted as places where one can find more to do than merely shop. Many have facilities for community activities and provide luxuriant vegetation, minizoos, art collections, and other varied exhibitions and entertainment. Yet, they seem no more likely than airports to provide urban dwellers with a genuine sense of community.

New Towns

Architects and planners have long been in the vanguard of the advocates of "new towns"; presumably, they could be among the clusters in Owen's regional city. In fact, more than forty new communities were completed or substantially begun in the United States during the 1960s. The two most notable—Columbia, Maryland and Reston, Virginia—are in the vicinity of Washington, D.C. Columbia occupies an area about the size of Manhattan; when completed in 1981, it is expected to have a population of 110,000. Land acquisition for Columbia involved 140 separate transactions and an average purchasing price of $1,500 an acre. A conscious effort has been made to bring quality and diversity to Columbia. A network of nonprofit institutions such as schools, health centers, libraries, and religious facilities has been responsible for attracting specialized schools and innovations in public education and health care. Reston has had difficulty in attracting residents and has been in danger of becoming a dormitory community rather than an independent center with its own economy, as originally planned. However, it may have turned the corner in these regards; if so, it will probably reach a population of 78,000 when completed. Whatever the success of the privately-developed new towns of the 1960s in becoming established communities, it nonetheless remains true that they typically are suburban housing and recreation developments. They have "not aimed at rectifying the poor housing and other disadvantages of low-income groups or at alleviating congestion by matching residential and industrial development . . . . Their size and location have been dependent on where it was possible to assemble the land, and their relation to the region has been only incidentally considered."[4]

The New Communities Act of 1968 authorized the secretary of the Department of Housing and Urban Development to guarantee the bonds, debentures, notes, and other obligations issued by new community developers to finance their projects. No such guarantee could be made until it was determined that the proposed new community would be economically feasible in terms of its economic base or potential for growth, and that it would contribute to the orderly growth and development of the area of which it is a part. The act required a plan, with appropriate time schedules, for financing land acquisition and land development costs of the proposed new community and for improving and marketing the relevant land. The act also called for a sound internal development plan for the new community; this plan was to give reasonable assurance that the development would contribute to good living conditions in the area being developed, would be characterized by sound land-use patterns, would include a proper balance of housing for families of low and moderate income, and would include or be served by satisfactory shopping, school, recreational, and transportation facilities. New communities eligible for assistance were not restricted with respect to either size or location. In the Housing and Urban Development Act of 1970, these aids were extended to public agencies, and the federal government agreed to guarantee payment of bonds issued for land acquisition, schools, and hospitals.

Jonathan, Minnesota, located about a half-hour drive by expressway from Minneapolis, was the first new town to benefit from the provisions of the 1968 act. It is expected to reach a population of 50,000. Among other similar new-town projects are Flower Mound (near Dallas); Maumelle (near Little Rock); Park Forest South (in Illinois); and Saint Charles (in Maryland).

Planned Unit Development (PUD)

Planned unit development (PUD) is yet another means to achieve cluster development. PUD is essentially a vehicle for packaging a mixture of residential, commercial, and industrial land uses on the same land tract. It permits increased flexibility in design, including the clustering and mixing of dwelling types; and it permits the garnering of public and common open space for the residents of the development. The land tract is developed as a whole and according to a plan. PUD exempts a development from detailed compliance with zoning rules if it is built in accordance with an approved plan.

Although PUD has been equated with the development of new towns, from the developer's point of view it is regarded as "an organic *part* of a town, be it old or new. For example, within Reston each village is in effect a PUD. Reston, when completed, will be a town, but within the village or PUD a resident can shop, play, go to school, and live in a multiplicity of housing types. Certainly a PUD is a better place to live than a subdivision."[5] Yet, it remains true that PUD, "despite the efforts of those who contributed to the models of existing enabling legislation, has not had a massive impact nationally."[6] Moreover, many of the criticisms that have been levelled against new towns apply equally to PUD.

New-Town Goals

In the face of declining birth rates, the argument that a large number of new towns will be necessary to accommodate future population growth loses much of its cogency. Even under the most optimistic forecasts for new town development, it is not likely that they would have any real impact on the national urban structure or contain more than a small fraction of the population. While some new-town proponents have maintained that "social balance" should be an objective in such projects, the prospect is not bright. The planned growth and high amenity levels advertised for some new towns have been interpreted by some to mean social exclusion. Indeed, there seem to be genuine strategic difficulties in trying to package numerous goals in one development form or program. This may further some types of coordination, but it increases the chance that feasible goals will be tied to infeasible goals. Mixing the goals of innovation and risk minimization is one example. Another is mixing economic and social needs with demand for private transportation and single family homes. At present, new housing for low-income families requires subsidies; the housing of the poor has largely come to them from the filtering process of the market. Since new towns would lack old housing, an enormous subsidy would be required to achieve social balance. But the urban majority are not likely to vote to subsidize new towns rather than existing cities. Moreover, there also is the danger that new towns will decrease access to opportunities, the heart of urban culture, by becoming nearly-closed subsystems of too small a scale. This would be true to the extent that new towns are removed from proximity to metropolitan areas. What is more likely, however, is that they will be near metropolitan areas, in which case they will not be able to maintain self-contained labor markets. Thus, with the exceptions of Columbia and Reston, most American new towns already show, apart from the process of development, little that distinguishes them from other suburban areas. A comprehensive review of the new-towns approach concludes that American developers are attempting to turn the notion that increased land values arising from urban development should be returned to the community into mere pursuit of private profit. The majority of developers' practices are

principally concerned with the physical and procedural aspects. Those public programs which have been established to date appear inadequate to further the satisfaction of the major objectives of the new town concept. And, finally, even if adequate public programs could be developed, such programs would be in pursuit of a number of highly questionable goals basic to the new town concept. Several of these goals are infeasible and irrelevant to the political, economic, and social structure of the modern metropolis, and in this respect the new town concept may well be an idea whose time has passed.[7]

Yet, even William Alonso, one of the harshest critics of new towns, acknowledges that they may play a useful role in testing and exhibiting innovations that might be adaptable to existing cities. However, the findings must be transferable to other areas, and the experiment must give a reliable indication of the probability that there will be success in the further applications of innovations. Evaluation and reporting must be objective, in contrast to the public relations output of most new-town advocacy, and findings must be made available promptly.[8] Certainly, there is much to be learned if both suburban developments and downtown urban renewal are to be planned and carried out so that they result in attractive places in which to live and work.

Linear Development

Another approach to concentrated development emphasizes linear development corridors, or axes, rather than cellular growth of the new town or PUD type. In the past the expansion of population and economic activity often followed a linear spatial path because of the influence of transportation routes. The paths of these axes were influenced primarily by geographical considerations. Growth of traffic along the original routes resulted in economies of scale and agglomeration. New technologies could be more readily incorporated into the existing infrastructure because the volume of traffic guaranteed their profitability. However, by lowering transport costs the resultant increase in traffic volume created added demand for still newer improvements. This cumulative process tended to concentrate and juxtapose various modes of transportation along the original major routes. Population, industry, and commerce clustered along these axes, which constituted extended, easily accessible markets attractive to new economic activity. Even agriculture in close proximity to development axes benefited relative to that in other areas because of its greater involvement in the dynamics of modernization and technological progress.[9]

The notion of developing high-accessibility corridors radiating out from the dominant urban core is, in fact, a common feature of the metropolitan plans adopted for numerous regions, including Washington, Baltimore, New York, Chicago, and Los Angeles. In some cases, e.g., Baltimore and Washington, and New York and Philadelphia, the corridors radiating from the respective cores are expected to coalesce, at somewhat higher densities than are presently found in the intercity areas. In most instances, one or more circumferential express highways are also provided, usually an outer belt and an inner belt. The resulting pattern encourages a spider-web structure of high-intensity traffic generators and, hence, high-density land uses, which is deemed to be more efficient than the sprawl which has typified so much of recent metropolitan growth.[10]

More ambitious uses of development corridors also have been proposed. Paul Ylvisaker, for example, believes that they could propel America into a new period of development for urban fringe areas.

The idea, simply put, is to encourage development to follow a dominating physical pattern of the land, as we did before with canals, railroads, highways, and airports. Utilities and services would be concentrated in "corridors" linking settlements. The first utility corridors could be placed between the settlement patterns into which we have lately gravitated, those along the coast with wedges driven into the Great Lakes area and other regions such as Atlanta and Denver. In this way, utility corridors would help to spread and thin our urban population in a linear fashion. At the same time, populations we have expected to concentrate in the urban fringe areas could cluster all along the utility corridors in pockets of higher density than the land has supported to date, a better solution by far than the half-serviced incremental development suffered by the outskirting open land of our cities.[11]

Clusters of Small Cities

Finally, little systematic attention has been given to the advantages and disadvantages of clusters of existing smaller cities that together may have the advantages of a larger city, while individually retaining those of smaller places.

Wilbur Thompson has noted that:

> A number of small and medium size urban areas, connected by good highways and/or other transportation facilities may form a loose network of interrelated labor markets. With widespread ownership of automobiles or a well-developed bus system, and with expressways permitting average speeds up to fifty miles an hour between home and work place, such a network could extend radially for twenty-five to thirty miles around one of the larger urban places or embrace a square fifty miles on a side and still be tied into a single, integrated local labor market. A half-dozen towns of, say, 25,000 population with two or three main industries each plus a dozen small one- or two-industry towns of half that size add up to a 300,000 population, extended local labor market, built on the moderately broad base of a couple of dozen separate industries. This federated local economy may achieve the minimum size necessary to [preserve] the collective existence of these smaller urban places.[12]

Clusters of small cities are found in numerous parts of the country. Thompson mentions the upstate Michigan Saginaw-Bay City-Midland area, and the Chapel Hill-Durham-Raleigh triangle in North Carolina. The North Carolina case could also include other Piedmont Crescent cities, such as Greensboro, Charlotte, Winston-Salem, and High Point. Still other examples are the Lower Rio Grande Valley in Texas, the Willamette Valley in Oregon, and the Kingsport-Bristol-Johnson City-Elizabethton area, in far eastern Tennessee and far western Virginia.

Integrated clusters of small cities and intermediate-size cities throughout the country have also been proposed as the bases for another approach to urban-development policy. This "growth-center" strategy will now be considered in some detail.

11 Urban Growth-Center Policy and Regional Development

Growth Centers

In Chapter 1 it was noted that urban economists are increasingly likely to turn their attention to the issue of a national growth policy, including the possibilities for decentralizing population and economic activity through the development of growth centers in presently stagnant regions of the country. The prestigious (though not equally influential) Commission on Population Growth and the American Future has, in fact, recommended such a strategy to "promote the expansion of job opportunities in urban places located within or near declining areas and having a demonstrated potential for future growth."[1]

There are several aspects of the growth-center approach that have obvious appeal to regional planners attempting either to slow the growth of large cities or to promote development in other areas, or both. First, a distinction may be made between spontaneous growth centers and induced growth centers.[2] The former are growing relatively rapidly as a result of natural forces, whereas growth of the latter is associated with government incentives and controls. If the spontaneous pattern of spatial resource allocation is deemed undesirable, then attempts can be made to alter it by inducing growth in alternative places.

Spread and Backwash Effects

If growth can, in fact, be induced in a center, how is this supposed to benefit the region concerned? Because the rationale of the growth-center strategy as a means for developing lagging areas depends on the existence of "spread effects," it is necessary to examine in detail the alleged nature of their generation and transmission.

Spatially, *spread* may be defined as the complex set of processes whereby the absolute level of development of a peripheral area is increased because of diffusion from a core area.[3] Although elements of the concept were recognized earlier, Albert Hirschman and Gunnar Myrdal are generally given credit for the first systematic treatment. (Although Hirschman used the term "trickle down," he noted that he meant by this precisely what Myrdal meant by "spread.") Hirschman argued that growth is communicated from the leading sectors of the economy to the followers, from one firm to another. The advantage of this approach "over 'balanced growth' where every activity expands perfectly in step with every other, is that it leaves considerable scope to *induced* investment decisions and therefore economizes our principal scarce resource, namely, genuine decision-making."[4]

Geographically unbalanced growth requires special consideration, for "while the regional setting reveals unbalanced growth at its most obvious, it perhaps does not show it at its best" because successive growth points may all "fall within the same privileged growth space."[5] The principal reason for the tendency for economic activity to become concentrated in one or a few growth poles is that the external economies associated with the poles are consistently overrated by investment decision-makers on the ground that "nothing succeeds like success." Thus, whereas a clustering of investment around the initial growth poles is beneficial at the beginning of development, it may be irrational at the later period. The actual effects of the growth points on their hinterlands depend on the balance between favorable effects that trickle down to the hinterlands from the progress of the growth points and the unfavorable, or polarization, effects on the hinterlands as a consequence of the attractiveness of the growth poles.

The most important trickling-down effects are generated by purchases and investments placed in the hinterlands by the growth points, though the latter may also raise the productivity of labor and per capita consumption in the hinterlands by absorbing some of their disguised unemployment. On the other hand, polarization may take place in a number of ways. Competition from the growth points may depress relatively inefficient manufacturing and export activities in the hinterlands, and the growth points may produce a "brain drain" from the hinterlands, rather than create opportunities for their underemployed and unemployed residents.[6]

Gunnar Myrdal's theory of circular causation, published at about the same time as Hirschman's analysis but developed independently, contains a number of notions that coincide with those of Hirschman. Myrdal found that whatever the reason for the initial expansion of a growth center, thereafter, cumulatively expanding internal and external economies would fortify its growth at the expense of other areas. These economies include not only a skilled labor force and better public facilities, but also a positive feeling for growth and a spirit of new enterprise.[7]

In developing his analysis, Myrdal employed the concepts of backwash and spread effects. The backwash effects involve the workings of population migration, trade, and capital movements. Like Hirschman, Myrdal noted the selective nature of migration from the hinterlands to the growth center, though he emphasized the fact that the young are the most prone to move. He also dwelt on the higher fertility rates of poor areas and their impact on the working-age group to total population ratio, which is likely to be relatively unfavorable in the hinterlands. Similarly, capital tends to flow to the growth centers because of increased demand. Consequently, incomes and demand increase again, resulting in yet another round of induced investment. The tendency to increased inequality is reinforced by the flow of savings from the hinterlands, where demand for investment capital remains relatively weak, toward the centers of expansion, where returns are high and secure. In addition, Myrdal recognized the critical significance of noneconomic factors in the perpetuation of poverty in the hinterlands. Their inability to support adequate health and education facilities, their generally conservative outlook—related to acceptance of the more primitive forms of tradition and religion—are all detrimental to the experimental and rational orientation of an economically progressive society.[8]

Among the spread effects, which may counter the backwash effects, are increased outlets for the hinterland's agricultural products and raw materials and a tendency for technical advance to diffuse from the growth centers. The spread effects will be stronger, the higher the level of economic development of a country. Moreover, the attractiveness of the growth centers may be weakened by increasing external diseconomies and high labor costs. Finally, the governments of the wealthier countries are likely to initiate policies directed toward greater regional equality.[9]

In spite of the similarities in approaches of Hirschman and Myrdal, there are considerable differences of emphasis. In particular, Hirschman seems to take for granted that strong forces eventually will create a turning point, once polarization effects have proceeded for some time. In any case, both approaches are primarily oriented toward problems of less-developed countries, and while the problems of lagging regions of industrialized countries may be similar to those of poor countries, they usually are certainly not so severe. For example, labor often is anxious to find employment and savings frequently are considerable, though they often flow to expanding regions rather than to local projects. And even in Appalachia, fertility rates are not very different from those in the United States as a whole.

Nevertheless, the persistence of interregional disparities in income and employment opportunities in industrial countries such as the United States poses special problems neglected by Hirschman and Myrdal. For example, even if central government policy does favor the development of lagging areas, a high proportion of public investment is financed by state and local governments. There is evidence from United States and Belgian data that current investment per capita by state and local governments is greatest in places that have had the most public investment in the past, so that even if the central government deliberately favors lagging areas, total public investment may, on balance, still favor more advanced areas.[10]

Economic Development Programs

The growth-center concept officially entered regional policy in this country with the Appalachian Regional Development Act and the Public Works and Economic Development Act. These acts, both passed in 1965 and both intended to stimulate development in lagging regions, stipulated that development projects should be concentrated in areas where there is a significant potential for future growth and where the expected return on public dollars invested will be the greatest. To give an indication of how this approach has worked out nationally, it is instructive to consider the experience of the Economic Development Administration (EDA), the agency created to implement the Public Works and Economic Development Act.

One of the principal features of the EDA program was the creation of multicounty Economic Development Districts (EDDs). It was recognized that individual distressed counties—termed "redevelopment areas" (RAs)—often lack sufficient resources to provide a solid base for their growth. However, because of economic interdependencies among adjacent areas, it was felt that economic development on a larger scale could be promoted by grouping together RAs and counties that were more healthy economically. EDA thus encouraged groups of counties—usually five to fifteen in number—to pool their resources for effective economic planning. Moreover, each EDD had to have a growth center, which was termed a redevelopment center if located in an RA, or a development center if located in another district county, which was usually the case. With the exception of the growth center, counties in the EDD were not eligible for project funding from EDA unless they were RAs. Nevertheless, all participating counties were expected to benefit from coordinated, district-wide development planning.

The rationale for EDA's growth center strategy is shown in the somewhat simplified illustration presented in Figure 11-1. The center's hinterland benefits from the spread of services, secondary jobs, and development expertise from the center, as well as from opportunities made available to hinterland residents who commute or migrate to the core. It may be noted that what one chooses to call a spread effect often depends on the particular perspective of the viewer. For example, from the perspective of County B in Figure 11-1, it is not clear that migration will be beneficial, whether the migrants go to the growth center in County E or leave the EDD altogether. If the migrants were unemployed *or* if unemployed workers with similar skills could replace the employed workers who migrate, the total output of County B would not or should not fall. Because the unchanged output is now divided among fewer people in County B, the average real per capita income will be higher than before. This may be regarded as a spread effect. On the other hand, the emigration of skilled workers who were employed in County B (or for whom employment would soon be found), and who were earning an income higher than the county average would result in a decline (or prevent as high a rise as otherwise possible) in the average real per capita income of the people remaining in County B and would also adversely affect the overall skill composition of its economy. This would be a backwash effect, in Myrdal's terminology.[11] Of course, if migrants from County B go to the district growth center, they may spend more of their earnings in County B than if they had migrated to more distant places. The leakage from County E would benefit County B but would obviously not affect the district. Finally, apart from these economic considerations are those of a political and social nature. Out-migration is often regarded as undesirable by people living in an area, whether or not the economic consequences are desirable for the people left behind. Here, too, the results would vary depending on whether one adopted the perspective of a single county, a single district, or a geographically wider frame of reference.

The notion of spread effects is most commonly associated with the induced generation of secondary jobs in hinterland counties such as County F in Figure 11-1. This is largely because of a pronounced tendency to identify the induced effects of an economic activity (growth pole) with *locally* induced effects (growth centers). However, the great weight of the empirical evidence indicates this view to be mistaken. For example, Beyers' analysis of interindustry purchases and sales relationships in the Puget Sound region showed that regional interindustry connections were weak compared with interregional interindustry relations. Value added and personal consumption were the most important regional linkages for many sectors. His data suggest that the usual conceptualization of a growth pole, "with its heavy emphasis on growth stimuli being transmitted via forward and backward interindustry linkages, is probably more applicable at a broad national level than at the small regional scale."[12] Gaile's growth-center test of the Milwaukee area led to the finding that "the concept of concentric 'spread' of growth from the 'growth center' has not been proven."[13] In another paper, Gaile reviewed 17 studies using the growth-center concept, and concluded that if a trend was discernible, it was that spread effects were either smaller than expected, limited in geographic extent, or less than backwash effects.[14] A study by Gray of the employment effect of a major new aluminum reduction and rolling mill at Ravenswood, West Virginia, 50 miles north of Charleston, found that the induced employment attributable to the plant's operations could be traced mainly to Ohio (power) and Louisiana (bauxite), but very little was discernible around Ravenswood.[15] Even more to the point in the

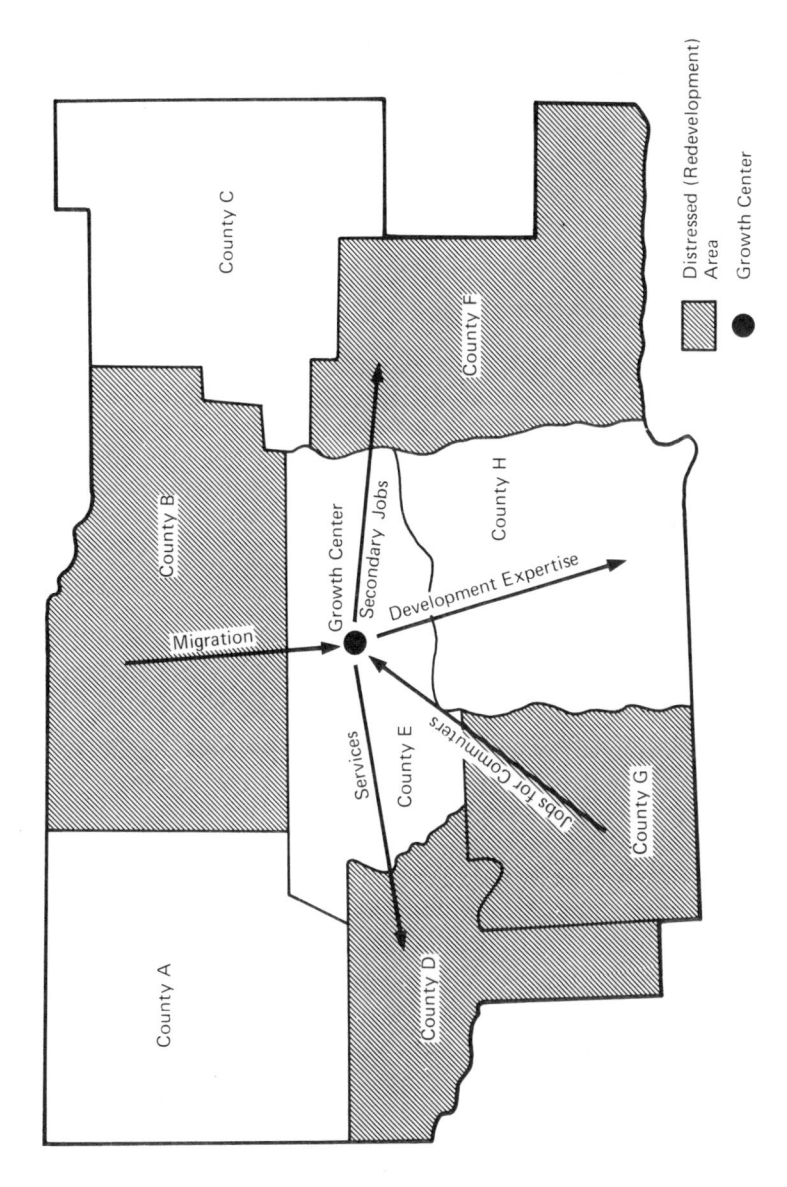

Source: Reprinted by permission of the publisher from Raymond H. Milkman, Christopher Bladen, Beverly Lyford, and Howard L. Walton, *Alleviating Economic Distress* (Lexington, Mass.: Lexington Books, D. C. Heath and Co., 1972), p. 126.

Figure 11-1. Economic Development Administration Development District and Growth Center Concepts

present context are the findings of a major internal evaluation of EDA's growth-center strategy:

On the basis of the twelve in-depth case studies conducted during the growth center evaluation, it is not yet clear that the growth center strategy outlined in the agency's legislation and expanded in EDA policy statements is workable. Residents of surrounding depressed counties designated as redevelopment areas received almost no employment or public service benefits from the EDA growth center projects surveyed by the evaluation team. Moreover, at the time of evaluation these projects had not resulted in more total job impact than similar projects placed in distressed areas, as had been suggested in the past.[16]

The same study also found that

the twenty-eight completed EDA projects in the growth centers analyzed showed no evidence of stemming out-migration from redevelopment areas or economic development districts. Less than 1 percent of the 850 employees surveyed at EDA-associated firms stated that they would have migrated from the area if their present job had not been available. The percentage of workers who indicated they would have moved to one of the nation's major metropolitan areas in the absence of the EDA-created job was even smaller.[17]

Those who evaluated the EDA growth-center strategy acknowledged that even though it was not producing the results that had been hoped for, this did not necessarily imply that a growth-center approach is unviable as a regional development strategy.

Dissatisfaction with EDA's growth-center approach also was reflected in a recent proposal to Congress for an Economic Adjustment Act to restructure federal programs for area and regional economic adjustment. The initial report in this regard reaffirmed the notion that "priority should be given to those areas with the greatest potential of providing higher productivity jobs for the underemployed, rather than attempting to create more productive jobs in all areas of high underemployment."[18] The report also was sharply critical of EDA's past performance.

The policy of dispersing assistance rather than focusing on those [areas] with the greatest potential for self-sustaining growth has resulted in much of EDA's funds going to very small communities. Over a third of its public works funds have gone to towns with less than 2,500 people, and over a half to towns with less than 5,000 population. There are relatively few kinds of economic activities which can operate efficiently in such small communities, so the potential for economic development in the communities is relatively small.[19]

The administration would like to abolish EDA; in its place, a system would be established in which the federal government would allocate funds to the states (who may choose to form multistate regional commissions but would be under no obligation to do so) after federal approval of state plans that outline how the funds would be used to assist distressed areas and prevent the creation of new distressed areas. While the states are given considerable planning latitude, there is no doubt that the federal government favors concentrating assistance in a relatively few areas to permit enough resources in one area to stimulate sustained growth.

Growth-Center Strategy

But even if designated growth centers could benefit from a growth-center strategy, it would appear on the basis of the evidence already discussed that the benefits would remain concentrated in them, with little impact on their distressed hinterlands. Thus, while there are no doubt many rural areas and small towns with unrealized economic-growth potential, a national growth-center policy to achieve rural development would probably be, on balance, not only economically inefficient, but also largely ineffective. However, this would not preclude a growth-center policy based on medium-size cities, ranging in size from say, 50,000 to 750,000 population—especially if they already have given some real evidence of possessing growth characteristics. In these centers, public funds may be integrated with actual or potential external economies to produce rapid growth with a minimum of external diseconomies. Although such centers do not need any government subsidy, it is easier to accelerate their growth than it would be to accelerate growth in a lagging region. However, the accelerated growth of intermediate growth centers should be made conditional on the granting of newly-created employment opportunities to a significant number of workers from lagging regions who could either commute or migrate. In cases where local unemployment rates are relatively high in spite of high growth rates, a policy of growth acceleration would also be made conditional on the employment of the local jobless.

What measures should be undertaken to implement a growth-center strategy along this line? The composition of the development aid tool kit, such as that now used by the Economic Development Administration, should be changed, since the tools would be applied to areas that are already economically healthy and growing, rather than to areas that have relatively poor growth prospects. There should be more emphasis on measures that would attract growing industries and less emphasis on subsidies whose principal appeal is to small firms in slow-growing, low-wage industries. There should be more money devoted to equipping relatively sophisticated industrial sites and less to building water and sewer lines (which may be sorely needed in rural areas, but which should not be a central concern of an agency whose purpose is to initiate self-sustained growth). The kinds of tools would have to be more varied and flexible than those presently applied in small towns and rural areas. The latter often need so many improvements to make them relatively attractive to firms, especially the bigger and more rapidly-growing ones, that whatever a development agency can do within the constraints of its limited resources is not likely to change greatly the total package of factors that a firm considers when making a location decision. On the other hand, the kind of growth centers proposed here would have a large variety of existing external economies. This means, in the first place, that a given type of aid extended by an economic development agency would not be so visible as it would be in a lagging area. However, if used wisely, a given type of aid can produce more employment opportunities in the growth center because it can be combined with these external economies. The development agency should seek out the bottlenecks that are hindering or preventing a firm from locating or expanding in the growth center and attempt to provide the assistance needed to overcome the resistance. The situation may call for a certain type of investment in amenities or in more directly productive infrastructure, or for a labor training subsidy, or for some combination of aid devices. Efforts also should be made to enlist the cooperation of prominent business leaders, as is now being done for job creation programs in the ghettos. In any case, it is essential that the aid be made conditional on the extension of job opportunities to persons from lagging regions (and in part to the unemployed and underemployed residents of the center).

The emphasis that is given here to the development of intermediate cities as the principal focus for a national regional policy is based not only on the job growth potential of these cities, but also on the fact that problems related to their growth are still amenable to solution. The massive renewal needs of large metropolitan areas can still be avoided by careful planning in growth centers. "A city of 'optimal size'" writes Benjamin Higgins, "must be big enough to be urbane in its range of activities for its residents, with the available technique of city planning and transportation."[20] Unless the government knows what places are going to grow it can provide public facilities only after the demand has appeared. If there is planned growth of a relatively few centers, then they can be provided with an integrated and coherent system of public facilities in advance of the demand.

Location Preferences

In recent years the Center for Economic Development of the University of Texas has investigated the location preferences of young people, primarily high school seniors, in various lagging regions. These persons represent the future leadership of their home areas; they also are at a stage in life where they must give at least relatively thoughtful consideration to various job, education, and residence alternatives. It is not possible here to discuss the subgroup break down in each case, or to consider the data collected on such factors as influence of friends and relatives on location preferences, locational expectations (as contrasted with preferences), and degree of responsiveness to wage differences. However, it may be useful to consider the results presented in Table 11-1.[21]

The data in Table 11-1 show, for all respondents in each area, the proportion who would prefer to live in each of three alternative places, assuming that they could earn the stipulated hourly wage. Interviews were held with numerous government and school officials in each area to determine what intermediate and large cities would be relevant to the survey respondents. In the results shown here, the large city options given to the Indians were Chicago, Los Angeles, or the San Francisco Bay area. For the other groups, they were Chicago and Detroit. The intermediate cities for Eastern Ken-

Table 11-1
Relative Frequency of Preferences for Home Areas, Intermediate Centers, and Large Cities, by Selected Groups of Young Persons

		Wage	Eastern Kentucky (1969)	Eastern Kentucky (1971)	Mexican Americans in South Texas	Southwestern Indians	Southwest Mississippi Blacks	Southwest Mississippi Whites
I	Home area	$1.50	64	69	75	43	65	74
	Intermediate center	1.50	26	24	15	29	15	21
	Large city	1.50	10	7	10	28	20	5
II	Home area	1.50	25	24	42	19	33	45
	Intermediate center	1.75	36	38	23	38	22	40
	Large city	2.00	39	37	35	43	45	15
III	Home area	1.50	18	16	31	17	20	28
	Intermediate center	2.00	40	40	34	38	30	54
	Large city	2.50	42	44	35	45	49	18
IV	Home area	1.50	10	14	21	16	16	18
	Intermediate center	2.25	36	37	38	33	27	56
	Large city	3.00	54	50	41	51	58	26
V	Home area	3.50	81	84	84	61	82	83
	Intermediate center	2.50	13	14	11	25	9	14
	Large city	1.50	5	3	5	14	10	3
VI	Home area	1.50	10	10	20	16	12	7
	Intermediate center	3.50	81	86	76	64	74	88
	Large city	2.50	9	4	4	20	14	5
VII	Home area	1.50	9	12	20	13	14	14
	Intermediate center	2.50	35	36	37	35	27	56
	Large city	3.50	56	52	43	52	59	30
VIII	Home area	1.50	6	9	14	15	8	8
	Intermediate center	3.50	27	27	30	32	18	45
	Large city	5.50	66	64	56	52	74	48

tucky were Lexington and Louisville; for the Mexican-Americans, San Antonio and Corpus Christi; for the Indians, Albuquerque; and for the Mississippians, Baton Rouge, Jackson, and Memphis.

It is evident that the mobility potential of these young people is quite high. Many would move even if there were no economic advantage (case I). Once there is any economic advantage at all to moving (case II), the proportion who would prefer to move varies from 55 per cent in the case of Mississippi whites to 81 per cent in the case of the Indians. In general, the preference patterns are clearly influenced by the structure of relative wages. With the exception of the Mississippi blacks, there is also a pronounced tendency for movers to prefer intermediate centers to large cities. This is perhaps best seen by contrasting cases VI and VII, which reverse the wages in the intermediate and large cities with that in the home community held constant.

While these findings do not necessarily apply to persons who have dropped out of high school or to older persons, they indicate that relatively more attention could be given in public policy to linking people in lagging areas to opportunities in intermediate centers. One of the most obvious means would be a permanent comprehensive relocation-assistance program. Moreover, on the basis of past experience, a great deal is known about how such a program should be set up and operated.[22]

Relocation Recommendations

I worked closely with the Commission on Population Growth and the American Future on questions of growth-center policy, human-resource development in lagging areas, and government-assisted migration, and concur in their finding that these approaches should complement one another. The Commission's position on growth centers was cited at the outset of this chapter. It is appropriate to conclude with their recommendations on rural human-resource development and comprehensive relocation assistance.

To improve the quality and mobility potential of individuals, the Commission recommends that future programs for declining and chronically depressed rural areas emphasize human resource development.

To enhance the effectiveness of migration, the Commission recommends that programs be developed to provide worker-relocation counseling and assistance to enable an individual to relocate with a minimum of risk and disruption.

Such programs should be designed to match an unemployed worker who is unable to find work locally with job opportunities elsewhere for which he is or can become qualified. Relocation counseling and assistance should not be designed to accelerate migration; rather, it should offer alternatives and facilitate the choice between remaining in a socially congenial and familiar location and moving to an economically healthier, if less familiar, place.

The program should include: (1) information about job opportunities in nearby urban centers; (2) pre-relocation supportive services, such as personal and family counseling; (3) employment interviews in potential destination areas; (4) coordination and assistance in the solution of problems involved in moving; and (5) post-relocation supportive services such as legal, financial, and personal counseling, and assistance to individuals and families in finding housing, schools and day-care facilities, and additional training opportunities.

In general, migration from declining areas is frequently ill-directed. It often involves a lengthy move to a distant city, with all the difficulties of adjustment. A superior approach may be to create new jobs nearer to or within the declining rural areas.[23]

12 Summary and Conclusions

Throughout history, cities have been criticized because of their size, density, form, and moral degredation. Yet, it has only been in the last generation that national governments have adopted or been implored to adopt explicit urban-growth policies. The impetus to do something about the urbanization process usually stems from three concerns. First is the widespread feeling that big cities are too big. Second is dissatisfaction with the structure of urban areas. Third is the notion that it is undesirable to have so many people leave nonmetropolitan areas to go to large cities. Often these points are presented as different aspects of a generally undesirable trend that has filled the central cities' ghettos with poor, unprepared migrants from rural areas and small towns, and has swelled the total populations of the larger SMSAs to the point where they are all but unmanageable. Only a few years ago, standard population projections were also indicating that if things were not bad enough already, they were certainly going to become worse, because the United States would have to accommodate 100,000,000 new people, or an increment amounting to about half the present population, before the end of the century.

Housing and Urban Development Act

In this context of an unprecedented national interest in coming to grips with the responsibility to find effective ways of guiding the spatial distribution of population and economic activity, Congress passed the Housing and Urban Development Act of 1970. The act declared that a national urban growth policy should be developed, and that it should (1) favor patterns of urbanization and economic development and stabilization that offer a range of alternative locations and encourage the wise and balanced use of physical and human resources in metropolitan and urban regions, as well as in smaller urban places with potential for accelerated growth;

(2) promote the continued economic strength of all parts of the United States, including central cities, suburbs, smaller communities, local neighborhoods, and rural areas; (3) help reverse trends of migration and physical growth that reinforce disparities among states, regions, and cities; (4) treat comprehensively the problems of poverty and employment associated with disorderly urbanization and rural decline; (5) develop means to encourage good housing for all Americans; (6) refine the goal of the federal government in revitalizing existing communities and encouraging planned, large-scale urban and new community development; (7) strengthen the capacity of general governmental institutions to contribute to balanced urban growth and stabilization; and (8) facilitate increased coordination in the administration of federal programs to encourage desirable patterns of urban growth and stabilization, the prudent use of natural resources, and the protection of the physical environment.

The act also provided for submission by the president to Congress of a biennial report on urban growth. The report should assist in the development of a national urban growth policy and provide information and data relevant to urban growth. It should also contain a discussion of urban problems and efforts being made at all levels of government to deal with them, as well as recommendations for programs related to national urban growth policy. The act authorized planning grants, at three-fourths of the relevant costs, to agencies responsible for formulating plans for determining where growth should take place in states, regions, and smaller areas.

At this writing, the bright hopes that may have been engendered by the act have been dimmed, if not extinguished. The first report on a national urban-growth policy was a watered-down compendium of data that implicitly denied the desirability of such a policy. The document obviously reflected the administration's lack of enthusiasm for any active federal role in shaping a national urban policy, and, conversely, its preference for state and local initiatives in such matters. But, in any event, the 1970 act was a rather poor guide for developing a national strategy. By promising something for everyone and failing even to hint at priorities, it could be as readily approved as most flag and motherhood bills. Indeed, by creating the appearance that an urban policy was in the process of being developed, the whole exercise may actually have retarded serious debate about, and the careful articulation of, an operationally feasible urban growth strategy.

Metropolitan Growth Pressures

Meanwhile, other events have also worked to reduce the public's sense of urgency concerning urban policy. The Great Society efforts of the 1960s may have been longer on rhetoric than ability to effect basic social and economic changes, and the degree to which benign neglect represents current socioeconomic policy may be overdrawn by liberal critics. Nevertheless, compared to the situation only six or seven years ago, there is less active concern today with respect to the problems of the central-city poor. Certainly, radical activism has dramatically abated; while the Patricia Hearst kidnapping in 1974 may have reminded the nation that poverty still exists, the resulting distribution of free food to the poor in response to the kidnappers' demands created little sympathy for their plight, and, in fact, may have had the contrary effect. Then, too, the middle classes, and particularly blue-collar workers and persons with relatively fixed incomes, feel they have their hands full trying to cope with the effects of inflation. Because changing attitudes toward marriage and the family have resulted in a low and declining birth rate, the issue of what to do with additions to the national population is now less acute than it appeared only a short time ago.

Whatever their merit in the past, arguments on behalf of measures to alleviate population growth pressures on big cities by subsidizing rural and small-town development are no longer very convincing; metropolitan growth is now primarily generated by natural increase within SMSAs. Moreover, the Bureau of Census, on the basis of a survey of 50,000 households taken from March 1970 to March 1973, reports that metropolitan areas are actually losing population as a result of migration flows. During the period in question, an estimated 4.6 million people left metropolitan areas, while 3.7 million moved in, for a net loss of 944,000. Although the growth of SMSAs has slowed, there has not been a reversal of the long-run trend toward increasing urbanization. A large part of the net movement from metropolitan areas represents urban development around the fringes of SMSAs. During the 1960s, employment in noncentral-city parts of SMSAs grew more rapidly than population. As jobs have increased in these areas, workers have found it easier to commute from communities just beyond the SMSA boundaries as defined in 1970. In keeping with the past, the survey indicated only a small migration of blacks to exurbia; of the 4.6 million out-migrants from SMSAs, only 188,000 were black.

The survey period was just before the beginning of the 1973-74 energy crisis. At this writing, the prospect of a long-term energy shortage seems assured, though perhaps it will not be as severe as it was during the period when the 1974 Arab oil embargo was in effect. Whether or to what extent the energy problem will cause more Americans to move back to the cities, or at least refrain from leaving them, is uncertain. In any event, a 1973 estimate placed the amount of open land being lost to urbanization at an area equal to the size of New Jersey every decade. This game can be played a number of ways. At the same rate of open-land consumption, it would require three centuries to take in an area the size of Texas, or about two centuries to take in an area equivalent to that of California. From one perspective, then, the nation would appear to be able to accommodate a considerably larger population and still have an enormous amount of open space left. On the other hand, most of the present population is concentrated on 10 per cent of the nation's area, on the Atlantic and Pacific coasts, around the Great Lakes, and in a few centers in between. The SMSAs in these areas are expected to continue their expansion in terms of people and area, so that by the end of the century they will have coalesced into extended urban regions. In this perspective, the issue of population growth in the "great open spaces" far from population centers may appear largely academic. Of course, the environments of distant places with highly attractive amenities, e.g., mountains and lakes, will continue to be threatened by the high and increasing demands of metropolitan residents for tourism, recreation, and second homes.

Urban Goals

I recently directed a study of public policy and regional development in nine Western nations, including the United States.[1] At the conclusion of my summary I suggested that the clearest generalization that could be drawn from the diverse experiences was that what is needed most from the whole range of persons concerned with regional policies is not hasty selection of general goals, but rather a better elucidation of what the problems really are. None of the eight colleagues who worked with me on the study questioned this finding, and several took the trouble to express their strong agreement. I believe that a similar judgment also is applicable in the present case.

There are certain general objectives and values to which the great majority of city dwellers would no doubt subscribe, at least in principle. For example, equality of opportunity, tolerance, and pluralism (within the limits of the law) are widely held to be desirable characteristics of American democracy at its best. However, the ways in which individuals and groups attempt to realize these goals in practice may, even if inadvertently, limit the degree to which others may realize them. Many, probably most, people prefer to live in affinity environments because of the sense of community they gain. And they are usually quite willing to let others have their own neighborhoods or quarters. In this sense pluralism and tolerance are served. However, in the past several decades middle-class whites have, at least implicitly, tended to identify opportunity and affinity environment with suburbia. Where the environment has been deemed particularly pleasant, strong sentiment (and in some instances even legal action) has been expressed in favor of local no-growth or highly-controlled growth policies. The economic consequences have become quite apparent.

Until fairly recently, the standard textbook definition of economics was the study of the allocation of scarce resources among competing uses in terms of "what, how, and for whom." The question of "where" did not seem to matter. The rapid emergence of urban and regional economics as distinct fields of study in the past dozen years is attributable to the importance of the "where" issue. The spatial distance separating the poor, the old, and racial minorities in the central cities from better housing, and more, better, and faster-growing employment opportunities in the suburbs cannot simply be assumed away. Urban renewal and attempts to refurbish the ghettos are not adequate responses, no matter how much good will may be involved. Ghetto residents need the freedom of choice to have their own affinity environments in the suburbs; otherwise, they do not have access to the full range of opportunities in the metropolis—and it is this access that is the heart of what cities are about. If substantial and sustained progress were made in this regard, it is likely that central cities could once again be made attractive to a broad spectrum of people. This, together with the energy crisis and an apparent taste among young adults for later marriage and fewer children could reverse the centrifugal tendency toward suburban sprawl; it could also do much to overcome existing needs and fiscal capacity imbalances between central cities and suburbs. But again, merely to state that these are desirable goals is no substitute for dealing constructively with problems that preclude their attainment.

Urban Problems

Even if conflicts between blacks and whites, the poor and the well-to-do, and central cities and suburbs were ameliorated to a significant extent, it might still be argued that the nation has an urban problem because the larger SMSAs and even larger urban regions are too big. The evidence considered in the foregoing chapters lends little support to this position. Crime and psychological stress are, or threaten to be, a part of the daily experience of many big-city residents, but these phenomena are related more to social and cultural problems than to city size. High levels of traffic congestion and air pollution are frequently cited as evidence that big cities are too big. Congestion, however, is more likely a reflection of underinvestment in transportation facilities and incorrect pricing of transportation services than of city size. For example, if a toll were imposed on vehicles using congested routes (the toll could be varied during the day in response to the degree of congestion), some drivers would use less congested routes, some would shift to public transportation or perhaps car pooling, some would shift away from peak-hour use of routes with tolls, and still others would abandon unimportant trips altogether. Similarly, polluters could be charged an effluent toll analogous to a congestion toll. The activity causing the pollution could be halted or moved away from the metropolitan area. More likely, however, would be a switch to a less-polluting process and the collection and treatment of harmful wastes. The latter, it may be noted, would not only improve resource allocation but might also increase city size, because collection costs are smallest in concentrated areas like large cities.

Public Preferences

In the urban economics literature it has been argued that an upward shift in the size of cities very likely corresponds to changes in public preferences over time. The reasoning is that rising incomes incline people toward a greater range of consumer choice, and rising levels of education result in greater specialization and, therefore, a need for a wider range of occupational choice. Conveniently, advances in technology, e.g., better transportation systems and improved means to control pollution, permit larger city sizes without significantly increasing congestion and pollution. With luck, the upward shift in preferred city size may even have approximated the 16.6 per cent increase in SMSA population between 1960 and 1970. The suggestion occurs elsewhere in the relevant literature that at least one very well-educated person, by his own admission, needs to live in a city of several million people so that he can find a score or so of kindred spirits. Life would simply be too stultifying in a smaller place. Presumably the more rapidly his erudition increases the more often he has to move.

However, even if one accepts the premises set forth in the preceding paragraph, it is not clear that they necessarily lead to the stated conclusions. In the first place, increasing levels of education should make it easier to find kindred spirits within any city of given size or growth rate. The cultural and intellectual amenities of big cities are undeniable, but care should be exercised not to exaggerate their importance. New York may offer 360 plays, concerts, and recitals in a given week, while a city of 600,000 population may offer only 18. Though the overall quality may be better in New York, the average person only has time to take in a fraction of the offerings in the smaller city. In spite of New York's wider range of choice, it would be difficult to argue that the cultural advantages of living there are 20 times greater than in the smaller city. Modern home entertainment equipment in particular has lessened the importance of living in a big city. Indeed, technological advances in telecommunications have tended to make access to cultural, scientific, and entertainment information and events less and less dependent on agglomeration. New York-based RCA, one of the world's leading telecommunications firms, recently ran an advertisement with the bold heading, "Is New York Really Necessary?" The answer was an unequivocal no.

Public preference surveys indicate that while the great majority of Americans do not want to live in big cities, most people do want relatively easy access to metropolitan (as well as nonmetropolitan) amenities and opportunities. Obviously, big cities are not going to wither, but their sizes and their structures are changing under the influence of technological, social, and economic forces whose results are not always readily predictable. There is little to be gained from trying to establish controls to curb the growth of cities. When such controls have been applied in Europe they invariably have been circumvented, and probably for very good reasons. In any event, the growth rates of the largest SMSAs have been slackening spontaneously, and there is good evidence that many are now declining in population and more will in the foreseeable future. It may thus appear ironic that so much belated concern is now being shown about controlling urban growth, but this is not necessarily the case. Many smaller- and medium-size SMSAs, particularly in the South and West, will continue to grow rapidly, as will many suburbs and exurban extensions of SMSAs in all parts of the country.

Urban Policy

I believe that it would be advantageous to have a flexible national urban growth policy; however, the many diverse points of view that would have to be reconciled make its realization in the near future unlikely, even though the whole issue will no doubt continue to stimulate a great deal of fancy rhetoric. Because of the great variety of patterns of urban change, there is much to be said for having urban policy formulated and implemented at levels below the federal government, although the latter may have to provide incentives and general guidelines to encourage state and local planning as well as to assure democratic participation in the planning process.

Urban economics cannot and should not bear the whole weight of urban growth policy formulation. Obviously there is a real need for more adequate decision-making procedures and institutions. In the absence of more effective means of governance, urban-growth policy will continue to be nothing more than the (mildly constrained) sum total of private decisions in the marketplace for land, with little regard for the effects of external consequences on the whole body politic.

An economist is no better equipped than anyone else to pronounce upon the nature of good government. Moreover, an optimum government or system of governments may be as elusive as an optimum-size city or system of cities. Nevertheless, it may be ventured here that some form of two-tier or multitier system of government is needed to deal effectively with problems ranging from the nature of a neighborhood park to metropolitan or regional transportation systems. At the very least, such approaches merit more experimentation. It has been argued in this volume that economic analysis has a valuable role to play in this process, indicating the likely intended and unintended consequences of alternative policies and programs. No attempt has been made to propose panaceas. Rather, emphasis has been placed on critical examination of the nature and significance of central urban policy issues. Problems of individual cities and metropolitan areas must be confronted on their own terms because they vary according to complex local interactions among urban size, growth, and structure. They also vary with such factors as region and age of city. For example, because many western cities have developed during an age of mass automobile ownership they tend to be relatively dispersed, making their people even more dependent on the automobile than people in older, more compact eastern cities.

In conclusion, then, I would like to stress again that the theoretical and empirical insights of economists can and should make important contributions to urban policy formulation. However, the quality of the decisions made also will depend heavily on the degree to which the local decision-making process with respect to the ends and means of urban policy is truly democratic.

Notes

Chapter 1
Introduction

1. Wilfred Owen, *The Accessible City* (Washington, D.C.: The Brookings Institution, 1972), p. 50.

2. John Friedmann, *Urbanization, Planning, and National Development* (Beverly Hills: Sage Publications, 1973), pp. 231-32.

3. Wilbur Thompson, "The Economic Base of Urban Problems," in Neil W. Chamberlain, ed., *Contemporary Economic Issues* (Homewood, Ill.: Richard D. Irwin, 1969), p. 2.

4. Harry W. Richardson, "A Comment on Some Uses of Mathematical Models in Urban Economics," *Urban Studies,* vol. 10, no. 2 (August 1973), p. 260.

5. Harvey S. Perloff, "The Development of Urban Economics in the United States," *Urban Studies,* vol. 10, no. 3 (October 1973), p. 297.

6. Niles M. Hansen, *Intermediate Size Cities as Growth Centers* (New York: Praeger, 1971).

Chapter 2
The Urban System of the United States

1. Reprinted with permission from Brian J. L. Berry, *Growth Centers in the American Urban System*, vol. 1 (Cambridge, Mass.: Ballinger Publishing Company, 1973), p. 11. Copyright © 1973 Ballinger Publishing Company.

2. Reprinted with permission from Berry, *Growth Centers in the American System,* vol. 1, pp. 11-15. Copyright © 1973 Ballinger Publishing Company.

3. Ibid., p. 17.

4. Wilbur Thompson, *A Preface to Urban Economics* (Baltimore: The Johns Hopkins Press, 1965), p. 24.

5. Reprinted with permission from Berry, *Growth Centers in the American Urban System,* vol. 1, p. 21. Copyright © Ballinger Publishing Company.

6. William Alonso, "The System of Intermetropolitan Population Flows," U.S. Commission on Population Growth and the American Future, *Population Distribution and Policy,* Sara Mills Mazie, ed., vol. 5 of Commission research reports (Washington D.C.: U.S. Government Printing Office, 1972), p. 327.

7. Ibid.

8. Peter A. Morrison, "Population Movements and the Shape of Urban Growth: Implications for Public Policy," in Ibid., p. 319.

9. Alonso, "The System of Intermetropolitan Population Flows," p. 328.

Chapter 3
Where Do People Want to Live?

1. For details on the methods involved, see Sara Mills Mazie and Steve Rawlings, "Public Attitude Towards Population Distribution Issues," U.S. Commission on Population Growth and the American Future, *Population Distribution and Policy,* Sara Mills Mazie, ed., vol. V of Commission research reports (Washington, D.C.: U.S. Government Printing Office, 1972), pp. 599-615.

2. Ibid., p. 607.

3. Ibid., pp. 612-13.

4. James J. Zuiches and Glenn V. Fuguitt, "Residential Preferences: Implications for Population Redistribution in Nonmetropolitan Areas," Ibid., p. 628.

5. Glenn V. Fuguitt and James J. Zuiches, "Residential Preferences and Population Distribution: Results of a National Survey," in *Where Will All the People Go?,* Report of the Subcommittee on Rural Development of the Senate Committee on Agriculture and Forestry, 93d Congress, 1st Session, October 23, 1973 (Washington, D.C.: U.S. Government Printing Office, 1973), pp. 21-41.

6. Ibid., p. 32. The emphasis is mine.

7. Ibid., p. 33.

8. Ibid.

9. Don A. Dillman, "Population Distribution Policy and People's Attitudes: Current Knowledge and Needed Research," unpublished paper prepared for the Urban Land Institute, October 15, 1973, p. 59.

10. James Q. Wilson, "The Urban Unease: Community vs. City," in H.J. Schmandt and Warner Bloomberg, Jr., eds., *The Quality of Urban Life* (Beverly Hills, Cal.: Sage Publications, 1969), p. 459.

11. George Gallup, Jr., "What Do Americans Think About Limiting Growth?" Speech given at the National Conference on Managed Growth, Chicago, September 16, 1973, p. 11.

12. Ibid., pp. 9-10.

13. Ibid., p. 12.

14. Ibid., p. 15.

Chapter 4
Some Limitations of Economic Models of Urban Growth

1. *The Daily Texan,* October 4, 1973, p. 4.

2. Benjamin Higgins, *Economic Development,* rev. (New York: W.W. Norton, 1968), p. 477.

3. Eric E. Lampard, "The Evolving System of Cities in the United States," in Harvey S. Perloff, and Lowdon Wingo, Jr., eds., *Issues in Urban Economics* (Baltimore: The Johns Hopkins Press, 1968), pp. 95-96.

4. E.A.G. Robinson, "Location Theory, Regional Economics and Backward Areas," in E.A.G. Robinson, ed., *Backward Areas in Advanced Countries* (New York: St. Martin's Press, 1969), p. 5.

5. Lloyd Rodwin, *Nations and Cities* (Boston: Houghton Mifflin, 1970), p. 18.

6. Harry W. Richardson, *Regional Growth Theory* (New York: John Wiley, 1973), p. 23.

7. Charles Tiebout, *The Community Economic Base Study* (New York: Committee for Economic Development, 1962).

8. Robert Spiegelman, *Review of Techniques of Regional Analysis with Particular Emphasis on Applicability of These Techniques to Regional Problems* (Menlo Park, Cal.: Stanford Research Institute, 1962), p. 30.

9. John Brazzel and Whitney Hicks, *Exports and Regional Economic Growth: A Comparison of the Economic Base and Staple Models* (Columbia, Mo.: University of Missouri, 1967), p. 6.

10. Richard Andrews, "Mechanics of the Urban Economic Base: Causes and Effects of Changes in the Base Ratios and the Base Ratio Elements (II)," *Land Economics*, vol. 31, no. 3 (August 1955), p. 248.

11. Ralph W. Pfouts, "An Empirical Testing of the Economic Base Theory," *Journal of the American Institute of Planners*, vol. 23, no. 2 (Spring 1957), pp. 64-69.

12. Edgar M. Hoover, "Some Old and New Issues in Regional Development," in E.A.G. Robinson, ed., *Backward Areas in Advanced Countries* (New York: St. Martin's Press, 1969), pp. 343-57.

13. Joseph J. Spengler, "Some Determinants of the Manpower Prospect, 1966-1985," in Irving H. Siegal, ed., *Manpower Tomorrow: Prospects and Priorities* (New York: Augustus M. Kelley, 1967), p. 91. See also J. Beaujeu-Garnier and G. Chabot, *Urban Geography* (New York: John Wiley & Sons, 1967), p. 162.

14. John Friedmann, *Regional Development Policy: A Case Study of Venezuela* (Cambridge, Mass.: The M.I.T. Press, 1966), p. 28.

15. Economic Development Administration, *Industrial Location as a Factor in Regional Economic Development* (Washington, D.C.: U.S. Government Printing Office, 1967), pp. 23-24.

16. Harvey S. Perloff, with Vera Dodds, *How a Region Grows* (New York: Committee for Economic Development, 1963), p. 24.

17. Hans Blumenfeld, "The Economic Base of the Metropolis," *Journal of the American Institute of Planners*, vol. 2., no. 4, (Fall 1955), 114-32.

18. Wilbur R. Thompson, "Internal and External Factors in the Development of Urban Economics," in Perloff and Wingo, eds., *Issues in Urban Economics*, p. 53.

Chapter 5
Advantages of the City

1. Ralph Turvey, "Side Effects of Resource Use," in Henry Jarrett, ed., *Environmental Quality in a Growing Economy* (Baltimore: Johns Hopkins Press, 1966), p. 47.

2. Werner Z. Hirsch, *Urban Economic Analysis* (New York: McGraw Hill, 1973), pp. 2-3.

3. Ibid., p. xvi.

4. Harry W. Richardson, "The Costs and Benefits of Alternative Settlement Patterns; Or Are Big Cities Too Big?" Paper prepared for the United Nations Symposium on Population Resources and Environment, Stockholm, September-October 1973, pp. 14-15.

5. Wilbur R. Thompson, "Internal and External Factors in the Development of Urban Economies," in Harvey S. Perloff and Lowdon Wingo, Jr., *Issues in Urban Economics* (Baltimore: Johns Hopkins Press, 1968), p. 53.

6. Ibid., p. 54.

7. Wilbur R. Thompson, "The Economic Base of Urban Problems," in Neil W. Chamberlain, ed., *Contemporary Economic Issues* (Homewood, Ill.: Richard D. Irwin, Inc., 1969), p. 8.

8. Ibid., p. 9.

9. Niles M. Hansen, *The Future of Nonmetropolitan America* (Lexington, Mass.: Lexington Books, D.C. Heath and Co., 1973).

10. Hirsch, *Urban Economic Analysis*, p. 22.

11. Allan R. Pred, "The Growth and Development of Systems of Cities in Advanced Economies," unpublished paper, p. 36.

12. William Alonso, "The Economics of Urban Size," *Papers of the Regional Science Association*, vol. 26 (1971), pp. 67-82.

13. Ibid., pp. 74-75.

14. Richardson, "The Costs and Benefits of Alternative Settlement Patterns," p. 16.

15. Alonso, "The Economics of Urban Size," p. 80.

16. Ibid., p. 81.

17. Robert E. Coughlin, "Attainment along Goal Dimensions in 101 Metropolitan Areas," *Journal of the American Institute of Planners*, vol. 39, no. 6 (November 1973), pp. 413-25.

18. Alonso, "The Economics of Urban Size," p. 67.

Chapter 6
When Is a Big City Too Big?

1. Wilbur R. Thompson, "Internal and External Factors in the Development of Urban Economies," in Harvey S. Perloff and Low-

don Wingo, Jr., *Issues in Urban Economics* (Baltimore: Johns Hopkins Press, 1968), p. 60.

2. René Dubos, "Promises and Hazards of Man's Adaptability," in Henry Jarrett, ed., *Environmental Quality in a Growing Economy* (Baltimore: Johns Hopkins Press, 1966), pp. 27-9, 38.

3. See Edward Higbee, *The Squeeze: Cities Without Space* (New York: William Morrow, 1960), pp. 9-10.

4. "Stress Is Called Population Curb," *New York Times*, September 22, 1963, p. 79.

5. Kingsley Davis, "The Urbanization of Human Population," in *Cities* (New York: Alfred Knopf, 1965), p. 23.

6. Graham Molitor, "Effects of Urban Overpopulation," in *Alternative Futures and Environmental Quality* (Washington, D.C.: Office of Research and Development, Environmental Protection Agency, 1973), p. 52.

7. Jean Gottmann, "Discussion," in Henry J. Schmant and Warner Bloomberg, Jr., *The Quality of Urban Life* (Beverly Hills, Cal.: Sage Publications, 1969), p. 77.

8. Jonathan L. Freedman, "Population Density, Juvenile Delinquency and Mental Illness in New York City," in U.S. Commission on Population Growth and the American Future, *Population Distribution and Policy*, Sara Mills Mazie, ed., vol. V of Commission research reports. (Washington, D.C.: U.S. Government Printing Office, 1972), pp. 511-23.

9. Daniel Stokols, "A Social-Psychological Model of Human Crowding Phenomena," Reprinted by permission of the *Journal of the American Institute of Planners*, vol. 38, no. 2 (March 1972), p. 74.

10. For a review of this literature see Paul Baum, *Issues in Optimal City Size* (Los Angeles: UCLA Graduate School of Management, 1971), pp. 22-25.

11. G. M. Neutze, *Economic Policy and the Size of Cities* (New York: Augustus M. Kelley, 1967).

12. Colin Clark, "The Economic Functions of a City in Relation to Its Size," *Econometrica*, vol. 13, no. 2 (April 1945), pp. 97-113.

13. Cited in Werner Hirsch, "The Supply of Urban Public Services," in Perloff and Wingo, eds., *Issues in Urban Economics*, p. 511.

14. Gordon Cameron, "Growth Areas, Growth Centres and Regional Conversion," *Scottish Journal of Political Economy,* vol. 17, no. 1 (February 1970), pp. 24-25.

15. E. A. G. Robinson, "Introduction," in E. A. G. Robinson, ed., *Backward Areas in Advanced Countries* (New York: St. Martin's Press, 1969), p. xvi.

16. For a more detailed version of this analysis see William Alonso, "The Economics of Urban Size," *Papers of the Regional Science Association,* vol. 36 (1971), pp. 67-83.

17. Lowdon Wingo, "Issues in a National Urban Development Strategy for the United States," *Urban Studies,* vol. 9, no. 1 (February 1972), pp. 16-20.

18. C. T. Haworth and D. W. Rasmussen, "Determinants of Metropolitan Cost of Living Variations," *Southern Economic Journal,* vol. 40, no. 2 (October 1973), pp. 183-192.

19. George S. Tolley, "Population Distribution Policy," Paper presented at the Conference on Public Policy Education, Custer, South Dakota, September 11, 1971.

20. Wingo, "Issues in a National Urban Development Strategy for the United States."

21. Wilbur R. Thompson, "The National System of Cities as an Object of Public Policy," *Urban Studies,* vol. 9, no. 1 (February 1972), p. 108.

22. Ibid.

Chapter 7
The Decline of the Central City

1. Neil N. Gold, "The Mismatch of Jobs and Low-Income People in Metropolitan Areas and its Implications for the Central City Poor," U.S. Commission on Population Growth and the American Future, *Population Distribution and Policy,* Sara Mills Mazie, ed., vol. V of Commission research reports (Washington, D.C.: Government Printing Office, 1972), p. 451. It is noteworthy that economic dispersal has not occurred because firms that are closer to the core have a higher propensity to move. "Instead this propensity is fairly constant over the entire metropolitan area. Since this percentage of firms being 'set loose' is relatively constant, the

shifting pattern of industrial location must result from the spatial pattern of destinations—the percentage of firms which 'set down' in each zone" (Leon Moses and Harold F. Williamson, Jr., "The Location of Economic Activity in Cities," *American Economic Review*, vol. 57, no. 2 [May 1967], p. 216).

2. Charles L. Leven, "Changing Sizes, Forms, and Functions of Urban Areas," in Ibid., p. 405.

3. John W. Dyckman, "Transportation in Cities," *Scientific American*, vol. 213, no. 3 (September 1965), p. 163.

4. John F. Kain and John R. Meyer, "Transportation and Poverty," *The Public Interest*, no. 17 (Fall 1969), p. 77-79.

5. Bennett Harrison, "The Once and Future City," *Challenge*, vol. 16, no. 4 (September-October 1973), p. 9. Reprinted with permission from *Challenge*.

6. Wilfred Owen, *The Accessible City* (Washington, D.C.: The Brookings Institution, 1972), pp. 51-52.

7. Kain and Meyer, "Transportation and Poverty," p. 86.

8. Ibid., pp. 84-87. There is evidence, based on data from Atlanta, that the accessibility of workers to jobs may not be as important in reducing inner-city underemployment as has been thought. In this view, "Underemployment could better be tackled through job training, placement, and child care programs than through new transit development." See Sanford H. Bederman and John S. Adams, "Job Accessibility and Underemployment," *Annals of the Association of American Geographers*, vol. 64, no. 3 (September 1974), pp. 378-386.

9. Gold, "The Mismatch of Jobs and Low-Income People in Metropolitan Areas and its Implications for the Central City Poor," p. 449.

10. Richard Muth, *Cities and Housing* (Chicago: University of Chicago Press, 1969), pp. 126-28.

11. John F. Kain, "Housing Segregation, Negro Employment, and Metropolitan Decentralization," *Quarterly Journal of Economics*, vol. 82, no. 2 (May 1968), pp. 175-97.

12. John F. Kain, "Housing Segregation, Negro Employment, and Metropolitan Decentralization: A Retrospective View," Harvard University Program on Regional and Urban Economics Discussion Paper no. 81 (May 1973).

13. Ibid., pp. 26-27.

14. Leven, "Changing Sizes, Forms, and Functions of Urban Areas," p. 406.

15. Charles Tiebout, "A Pure Theory of Local Expenditures," *Journal of Political Economy,* vol. 64, no. 5 (October 1956), pp. 416-24.

16. Wallace E. Oates, "The Effects of Property Taxes and Local Public Spending on Property Values: An Empirical Study of Tax Capitalization and the Tiebout Hypothesis," *Journal of Political Economy,* vol. 77, no. 6 (November-December 1969), p. 709.

17. Leven, "Changing Sizes, Forms, and Functions of Urban Areas," p. 406.

18. Harrison, "The Once and Future City," p. 9. Reprinted with permission from *Challenge*.

19. Roy W. Bahl, "Metropolitan Fiscal Structures and the Distribution of Population Within Metropolitan Areas," in U.S. Commission on Population Growth and the American Future, *Population Distribution and Policy,* p. 428.

20. Alan K. Campbell and Seymour Sacks, *Metropolitan America: Fiscal Patterns and Governmental Systems* (New York: The Free Press, 1967).

21. Bahl, "Metropolitan Fiscal Structures and the Distribution of Population Within Metropolitan Areas," p. 430.

22. Ibid., pp. 429-30.

23. C. Lowell Harriss, "Property Taxation: What's Good and What's Bad," *Challenge,* vol. 16, no. 4 (September-October 1973), pp. 16-21.

24. Ibid.

25. Bahl, "Metropolitan Fiscal Structures and the Distribution of Population Within Metropolitan Areas," p. 439.

26. Marjorie Cahn Brazer, "Economic and Social Disparities Between Central Cities and Their Suburbs," *Land Economics,* vol. 43, no. 3 (August 1967), p. 300.

27. Ibid.

28. Don A. Dillman, "Population Distribution Policy and People's Attitudes: Current Knowledge and Needed Research," unpublished paper prepared for the Urban Land Institute, October 15, 1973, p. 28.

29. Robert L. Wilson, "Livability of the City: Attitudes and Urban Development," in F. Stuart Chapin, Jr. and Shirley F. Weiss, eds., *Urban Growth Dynamics* (New York: John Wiley and Sons, 1962), pp. 359-99.

30. Ibid., p. 398.

31. John Gulick, Charles E. Bowerman, and Kurt W. Back, "Newcomer Enculturation in the City: Attitudes and Participation," in Ibid., pp. 356-57.

32. Rupert B. Vance, *Human Geography of the South* (Chapel Hill, N.C.: University of North Carolina Press, 1932), p. 507.

Chapter 8
The Central City Neighborhood

1. Lewis Mumford, *The Culture of Cities* (New York: Harcourt, Brace and Company, 1938), p. 488.

2. John Friedmann, "The Future of the Urban Habitat," in Donald M. McAllister, ed., *Environment: A New Focus for Land-Use Planning* (Washington, D.C.: NSF, October 1973), p. 64.

3. Ibid., p. 64.

4. Richard Lamanna, "Value Consensus Among Urban Residents," *Journal of the American Institute of Planners*, vol. 30, no. 4 (November 1964), pp. 317-23.

5. Herbert J. Gans, "The Balanced Community: Homogeneity or Heterogeneity in Residential Areas?" *Journal of the American Institute of Planners*, vol. 27, no. 3 (August 1961), p. 182.

6. Anthony Downs, "The Future of American Ghettos," Paper presented at the American Academy of Arts and Sciences Conference on Urbanism, Cambridge, Mass., October 27-28, 1967, p. 7.

7. Ibid., pp. 7-8.

8. Charles M. Barresi, "Racial Transition in an Urban Neighborhood," *Growth and Change*, vol. 3, no. 3 (July 1972), pp. 16-22.

9. Ibid., p. 20.

10. David Harvey, "Society, the City and the Space-Economy of Urbanism," Commission on College Geography Resource Paper no. 18 (Washington, D.C.: Association of American Geographers, 1972), p. 11.

11. James Q. Wilson, "The Urban Unease: Community vs. City," in Henry J. Schmandt and Warner Bloomberg, Jr., *The Quality of Urban Life* (Beverly Hills, Calif.: Sage Publications, 1969), p. 465.

12. Theodore Drettboom Jr., Ronald J. McAllister, Edward J. Kaiser, and Edgar W. Butler, "Urban Violence and Residential Mobility," *Journal of the American Institute of Planners*, vol. 37, no. 5 (September 1971), pp. 319-25.

13. Stanislav V. Kasl and Ernest Harburg, "Perceptions of the Neighborhood and the Desire to Move Out," *Journal of the American Institute of Planners*, vol. 38, no. 5 (September 1972), pp. 318-24.

14. James Heilbrun, *Urban Economics and Public Policy* (New York: St. Martin's Press, 1974), p. 259.

15. Eric G. Moore, "Residential Mobility in the City," Commission on College Geography Resource Paper No. 13 (Washington, D.C.: Association of American Geographers, 1972), p. 45.

16. Heilbrun, *Urban Economics and Public Policy*, p. 259.

17. Ibid., p. 260.

18. Ibid., p. 280.

19. Wilson, "The Urban Unease: Community vs. City," pp. 463-64.

20. Ibid., pp. 464-65.

21. Heinz Kohler, *Economics and Urban Problems* (Lexington, Mass.: D.C. Heath and Co., 1973), p. 284.

22. Ibid., p. 307.

23. Wilson, "The Urban Unease: Community vs. City," p. 466.

24. Ibid., pp. 466-67.

25. Wilbur R. Thompson, "The Economic Base of Urban Problems," in Neil W. Chamberlain, ed., *Contemporary Economic Issues* (Homewood, Ill.: Richard D. Irwin, 1969), p. 38.

26. John F. Kain and Joseph J. Persky, "Alternatives to the Gilded Ghetto," Harvard University Program on Regional and Urban Economics Discussion Paper No. 21 (February 1968), pp. 18-19.

27. Ibid., pp. 19-25.

28. Downs, "The Future of American Ghettos," pp. 28-30.

29. Ibid., p. 29.

Chapter 9
The Growth Controversy in the Suburbs

1. Rand Urban Policy Analysis Group, "Alternative Growth Strategies for San Jose: Initial Report of the Rand Urban Policy Analysis Project," A working note prepared for the National Science Foundation (Santa Monica, Cal.: Rand Corporation, October 1971), p. vi.

2. Richard E. Slitor, *The Federal Income Tax in Relation to Housing*, National Commission on Urban Problems Research Report No. 5 (Washington, D.C.: U.S. Government Printing Office, 1968), pp. 16-20.

3. *Wall Street Journal*, November 27, 1970, p. 1.

4. Earl Finkler, *Nongrowth as a Planning Alternative: A Preliminary Examination of an Emerging Issue*, American Society of Planning Officials Planning Advisory Service Report No. 283 (September 1972), p. 33.

5. Ibid.

6. Wilbur R. Thompson, "Problems That Sprout in the Shadow of No-Growth," Reprinted with permission from the *American Institute of Architects Journal* (December 1973), reprint without page numbers. Copyright 1973 The American Institute of Architects.

7. Jon Nordheimer, "Rich Boca Resolves to Stop Growing," *New York Times*, February 9, 1973, p. 37.

8. Ibid.

9. Thompson, "Problems That Sprout in the Shadow of No-Growth." Reprinted with permission from the *AIA Journal*, December 1973. Copyright 1973 The American Institute of Architects.

10. Michael A. Agelasto, II, "No-Growth and the Poor," *Planning Comment*, vol. 9, nos. 1-2 (Spring 1973), pp. 6-7.

11. Thompson, "Problems That Sprout in the Shadow of No-Growth." Reprinted with permission from the *AIA Journal*, December 1973. Copyright 1973 The American Institute of Architects.

12. Mancur Olsen, *The Logic of Collective Action* (Cambridge: Harvard University Press, 1965), p. 128.

13. Robert L. Bish, "Economic Analysis and Metropolitan Organization: Commentary," *Journal of the American Instutute of Planners*, vol. 39, no. 6 (November 1973), p. 410.

14. David K. Hartley, Milton Patton, and Ralph R. Widner, "Experiments in Growth Policy," discussion paper prepared for the Department of Housing and Urban Development (Columbus, Ohio: Academy for Contemporary Problems, 1973), pp. 88-89.

Chapter 10
Cluster Development

1. Edgar M. Hoover, *An Introduction to Regional Economics* (New York: Alfred A. Knopf, 1971), p. 111.

2. Wilfred Owen, *The Accessible City* (Washington, D.C.: The Brookings Institution, 1972), pp. 112-13.

3. Ibid., pp. 58-59.

4. Ibid., pp. 78.

5. Gerald C. Finn, "Comments," in Robert W. Burchell, ed., *Frontiers of Planned Unit Development* (New Brunswick, N.J.: Rutgers University Center for Urban Policy Research, 1973), p. 287.

6. George Sternlieb, et al., "Planned Unit Development: A Summary of Necessary Considerations," in Ibid., p. 303.

7. James A. Clapp, *New Towns and Urban Policy* (New York: Dunellen, 1971), p. 287.

8. William Alonso, "The Mirage of New Towns," *The Public Interest*, no. 19 (Spring 1970), pp. 16-17.

9. P. Pottier, "Axes de communication et théorie de développement," *Revue économique*, vol. 14 (January 1963), pp. 70-114.

10. Harold K. Meyer, *The Spatial Expression of Urban Growth* (Washington, D.C.: Association of American Geographers, Commission on College Geography, Resource Paper No. 7, 1969), p. 49.

11. Paul N. Ylvisaker, "Density in the Urban Fringe Area," in *Density: Five Perspectives* (Washington, D.C.: Urban Land Institute, 1972), p. 20.

12. Wilbur Thompson, *A Preface to Urban Economics* (Baltimore: Johns Hopkins Press, 1965), p. 34.

Chapter 11
Urban Growth-Center Policy and Regional Development

1. Commission on Population Growth and the American Future, *Population and the American Future* (New York: New American Library, 1972), p. 223.

2. William Alonso and Elliott Medrich, "Spontaneous Growth Centers in Twentieth-Century American Urbanization," in Niles M. Hansen, *Growth Centers in Regional Economic Development* (New York: Free Press, 1972), pp. 229-65.

3. Gary L. Gaile, "Notes on the Concept of 'Spread,'" unpublished paper, Department of Geography, UCLA, 1973, p. 1.

4. Albert O. Hirschman, *The Strategy of Economic Development* (New Haven: Yale University Press, 1958), pp. 62-63.

5. Ibid., p. 184.

6. Ibid., pp. 187-90.

7. Gunnar Myrdal, *Rich Lands and Poor* (New York: Harper and Brothers, 1957), pp. 23-7.

8. Ibid., pp. 27-31.

9. Ibid., pp. 31-3.

10. Niles M. Hansen, "Unbalanced Growth and Regional Development," *Western Economic Journal*, vol. 4, no. 1 (Fall 1965), pp. 3-14; and Niles M. Hansen, "The Structure and Determinants of Local Public Investment Expenditures," *Review of Economics and Statistics*, vol. 47, no. 2 (May 1965), pp. 150-62.

11. Dominick Salvatore, "The Operation of the Market Mechanism and Regional Inequality," *Kyklos*, vol. 25, no. 3 (1972), pp. 518-36.

12. William B. Beyers, "Growth Centers and Interindustry Linkages," unpublished paper, Department of Geography, University of Washington, Seattle.

13. Gary L. Gaile, "Growth Center Theory: An Analysis of its Formal Spatial-Temporal Aspects," unpublished paper presented at the Southern California Academy of Sciences Annual Meeting, Long Beach, May 5, 1973, p. 12.

14. Gaile, "Notes on the Concept of 'Spread,'" p. 15.

15. Irwin Gray, "Employment Effect of a New Industry in a Rural Area," *Monthly Labor Review*, vol. 92, no. 6 (June 1969), p. 29.

16. Raymond H. Milkman, Christopher Bladen, Beverly Lyford, and Howard L. Walton, *Alleviating Economic Distress* (Lexington, Mass.: Lexington Books, D. C. Heath and Co., 1972), p. 204.

17. Ibid., p. 206.

18. Report to the Congress on the Proposal for an Economic Adjustment Program (Washington, D.C.: Department of Commerce and the Office of Management and Budget, February, 1974), p. 10.

19. Ibid., p. 25.

20. Benjamin Higgins, *Economic Development*, rev. ed. (New York: W. W. Norton, 1968), p. 468.

21. The eastern Kentucky respondents were all high school seniors in the five-county Big Sandy region. The Mexican-Americans were high school juniors and seniors and young MDTA trainees in the Rio Grande Valley of Texas. The Indians were high school seniors belonging to the Navajo, Zuni, and Rio Grande Pueblo tribes. The Mississippi respondents were high school seniors in Amite, Jefferson, Pike, and Walthall counties. For more detailed analyses see Niles M. Hansen, *Location Preferences, Migration, and Regional Growth* (New York: Praeger, 1973).

22. Ibid.

23. Commission on Population Growth and the American Future, *Population and the American Future*, pp. 222-23.

Chapter 12
Summary and Conclusions

1. Niles M. Hansen, *Public Policy and Regional Economic Development: The Experience of Nine Western Countries* (Cambridge, Mass.: Ballinger, 1974).

Index

Index

Adams, John S., 160
Agelasto, Michael A. II, 164
Agriculture, 10, 25, 125-126
Albuquerque, New Mexico, 141
Alonso, William, 18, 46, 47, 55, 57, 125, 154, 157, 159, 165, 166
Amenities, 38, 42, 45, 149
Anaheim, California, 64
Andrews, Richard, 156
Appalachia, 62, 99
Atlanta, Georgia, 126
Austin, Texas, 31
Australia, 53

Back, Kurt W., 162
Backwash effects, 129-136
Bahl, Roy, 77, 80, 161
Baltimore, Maryland, 126
Barresi, Charles, 162
Baton Rouge, Louisiana, 141
Baum, Paul, 158
Bederman, Sanford, 160
Berry, Brian J. L., 9, 11, 13, 14, 16, 25, 44, 153
Beyers, William, 134, 166
Bish, Robert L., 165
Bladen, Christopher, 167
Bloomberg, Warner, Jr., 155, 158, 163
Blumenfeld, Hans, 156
Boca Raton, Florida, 108-109
Boulder, Colorado, 109
Bowerman, Charles E., 162
Brazer, Majorie Cahn, 82, 161
Brazzel, John, 155
Burchell, Robert W., 165
Bureau of Economic Analysis, U.S. Department of Commerce, 9
Butler, Edgar W., 163

Cameron, Gordon, 53, 159
Campbell, Alan K., 78, 161
Canada, 53
Central place theory, 37, 117-119
Chamberlain, Neil, 157
Chapin, F. Stuart, Jr., 162
Chicago, Illinois, 76, 126, 139
Christian, John, 50
Clapp, James A., 165
Clark, Colin, 53, 158
Cleveland, Ohio, 64, 93, 96
Columbia, Maryland, 122, 124

Commission on Population Growth and the American Future, 15, 19, 23, 52, 129, 141-142
Communications, 45, 149
Commuting, 9-10, 23, 146
Corpus Christi, Texas, 141
Costs of government services, 52-58
Coughlin, Robert, 157
Crime, 27, 50-52, 53, 90-94, 148

Daily Urban Systems (DUSs), 9-15, 24-25, 27
Dallas, Texas, 64, 83, 121, 123
Davis, Kingsley, 50, 158
Density gradients, 24-25
Denver, Colorado, 109, 126
Detroit, Michigan, 64, 76, 91, 139
Dillman, Don A., 154, 161
Dodds, Vera, 156
Downs, Anthony, 89, 99, 162, 163
Drettboom, Theodore, Jr., 163
Dubos, René, 50, 158
Durham, North Carolina, 83-85
DUSs. *See* Daily Urban Systems
Dyckman, John W., 160

Economic base analysis, 33-39
Economic Development Administration, 132-137
Employment change: in central cities, 65, 69-72, 75-76; in suburbs, 65, 69-72, 75-76, 106-107; and growth centers, 137-139
Energy, 74, 146, 148
Entrepreneurship, 42-43, 45
Environmental protection, 63, 111-113, 146-149
External diseconomies, 40, 49, 57-58, 131
External economies, 38, 41-42, 46, 49, 57-58, 72, 125, 131, 138

Fairfax County, Virginia, 112
Family, 45, 145, 148
Finkler, Earl, 103, 164
Finn, Gerald C., 165
Fiscal disparities. *See* Tax policies
Fort Lauderdale, Florida, 107
Freedman, Jonathan, 158
Friedmann, John, 153, 156, 162
Fuguitt, Glenn, 23, 25, 154

171

Gaile, Gary L., 134, 166
Gallup, George, Jr., 29, 155
Gallup poll, 27-29, 51
Gans, Herbert J., 162
German Federal Republic, 46
Ghetto. *See* Neighborhood
Gold, Neil M., 69, 70, 71, 159, 160
Gottman, Jean, 50, 158
Gould, Glenn, 45
Government programs: for central cities, 94-97; for metropolitan areas, 112; state policies, 112-113; and new towns, 122-123; for lagging regions, 132-137. *See also* National urban policy
Government sector, 11, 112
Grant, W. Horsley, 50
Gravity models, 37
Gray, Irwin, 134, 167
Great Plains, 62
Greensboro, North Carolina, 83-85
Growth centers, 4, 6, 129-142
Growth theory, 3
Gulick, John, 162

Hansen, Niles M., 44, 153, 157, 166, 167
Harburg, Ernest, 163
Harrison, Bennett, 73, 77, 160, 161
Harriss, C. Lowell, 161
Hartley, David K., 165
Harvey, David, 91, 162
Haworth, Charles, 58, 159
Heilbrun, James, 163
Hicks, Whitney, 155
Higbee, Edward, 158
Higgins, Benjamin, 32, 139, 155, 167
Hirsch, Werner, 41, 156, 158
Hirschman, Albert, 130-132, 166
Hoover, Edgar M., 156, 165
Housing markets, 71, 75-76, 92-93, 98-99, 109-113, 124
Houston, Texas, 64, 83, 107, 121

Income and city size, 44, 46-48, 55-61
Industrial complex analysis, 37
Industrial filtering, 43-44
Information, 44-45
Innovation, 40, 42-45, 46, 124
Input-output analysis, 37
Isard, Walter, 32

Jackson, Mississippi, 141
Japan, 46
Jarrett, Henry, 156, 158

Kain, John, 75, 76, 98, 160, 163
Kaiser, Edward J., 163

Kasl, Stanislav V., 163
Kohler, Heinz, 163

Lamanna, Richard, 162
Lamm, Richard D., 51, 54
Lampard, Eric, 32, 155
Langner, Thomas, 50
Leven, Charles L., 160, 161
Lexington, Kentucky, 141
Limitation of growth, 25, 31, 101-115
Location preferences, 18-29, 60-61, 83-85, 139-141, 149-150
Location quotient, 35
Location theory, 32-33
London, England, 53, 88
Los Angeles, California, 64, 126, 139
Lösch, August, 32
Louisville, Kentucky, 141
Lyford, Beverly, 167

Manufacturing, 11, 43, 65, 130
Mazie, Sara Mills, 17, 20, 21, 22, 80, 154, 158, 159
McAllister, Ronald J., 163
Medrich, Elliott, 165
Megalopolis, 50
Memphis, Tennessee, 96, 141
Meyer, Harold K., 165
Meyer, John R., 160
Miami, Florida, 64, 83, 108
Migration, 11, 15, 16, 43, 58, 60, 62, 130-136, 141-142, 145-146
Milkman, Raymond H., 167
Milwaukee, Wisconsin, 134
Molitor, Graham, 50, 158
Moore, Eric G., 163
Morrison, Peter, 154
Moses, Leon, 160
Mumford, Lewis, 162
Muth, Richard, 160
Myrdal, Gunnar, 130-132, 166

National urban policy, 3, 6, 63, 129, 143-145, 150-151
Neighborhood: attitudes toward, 26-28, 91; and affinity environment, 88-90, 119, 147; change process in, 90; ghetto, 90-100, 147-148
Neoclassical regional growth theory, 32-33
Neutze, G. M., 53, 158
Newark, New Jersey, 64
New Mexico, 107-108
New Orleans, Louisiana, 96
New towns, 4, 121-125
New York City, 52, 60, 92-93, 96, 126, 149
Nonmetropolitan areas: population change, 8, 62; proximity to metropolitan areas,

23-26, 47; and industrial filtering, 43-44; attitudes toward population density, 49-51; and poverty, 64-65, 68
Nordheimer, Jon, 164

Oates, Wallace, 161
Olsen, Mancur, 164
Optimum city size, 48, 59-61
Oregon, 107
Owen, Wilfred, 1, 120, 121, 153, 160, 165

Patton, Milton, 165
Perloff, Harvey S., 153, 155, 156, 157, 158
Persky, Joseph, 98, 163
Petaluma, 110-111
Pfouts, Ralph, 156
Philadelphia, Pennsylvania, 126
Pickard, Jerome, 15
Piedmont Crescent, 83, 85, 127
Pittsburgh, Pennsylvania, 64
Planned unit development, 123
Planning, 6, 18, 29, 32, 47, 63, 112-115, 124-125
Policy. *See* National urban policy
Population density, 49-52
Population growth: in the United States, 7-8, 15, 18, 145-146; in metropolitan areas, 7-8, 18, 62, 64-67, 150; in Daily Urban Systems, 10-11, 14; projections for urban regions, 15, 17; attitudes toward, 20-23; and effective demand, 46; and urban problems, 61-62, 103-104
Pottier, P., 165
Poverty, 46-47, 53, 64-65, 68
Pred, Allan, 157
Proximity, 41, 45, 47, 49, 72
Puget Sound, 134

Racial composition: in central cities, 7-8, 64-67; in suburbs, 7-8, 64-67
Ramapo Plan, 108, 111
Rasmussen, David, 58, 159
Rawlings, Steve, 20, 21, 22, 154
Relocation policy, 141-142
Reston, Virginia, 122-124
Richardson, Harry, 3, 41, 153, 155, 157
Robinson, E. A. G., 32, 55, 155, 156, 159
Rodwin, Lloyd, 155
Rural areas. *See* Nonmetropolitan areas

Sacks, Seymour, 78, 80, 161
St. Louis, Missouri, 64, 92-93
Salvatore, Dominick, 166
San Antonio, Texas, 96, 141
San Diego, California, 64
San Francisco Bay region, 110, 139

San Jose, California, 104
Schmandt, Henry J., 155, 158, 163
Shift-share analysis, 37
Siegal, Irving, 156
Simulation, 4-5
Slitor, Richard E., 164
SMSAs. *See* Standard Metropolitan Statistical Areas
South, 53, 64-65, 82-86, 150
Spengler, Joseph, 156
Spiegelman, Robert, 155
Spread effects, 129-137
Standard Metropolitan Statistical Areas (SMSAs): defined, 7, 9; coalescence of, 120, 146
Sternlieb, George, 165
Stokols, Daniel, 52, 158

Tax policies, 76-82, 104-105, 112, 148
Technology, 2, 44-45, 73, 149
Tertiary sector, 11, 38-39, 44-45, 119
Thompson, Wilbur, 3, 10, 39, 42, 43, 44, 109, 113, 127, 153, 156, 157, 159, 163, 164, 165
Tiebout, Charles, 77, 79, 155, 161
Tolley, George, 59, 159
Transportation, 38-39, 42, 49, 71-75, 96, 98, 104, 113, 114, 117, 119-121, 126-127, 148, 151
Turvey, Ralph, 156

Unbalanced growth, 130
Union wage policy, 60
Urban hierarchy, 37, 43
Utility corridors, 126

Vance, Rupert, 85, 162

Walton, Howard L., 167
Washington, D.C., 64, 96, 112, 122, 126
Weber, Alfred, 32
Weiss, Shirley F., 162
Widner, Ralph R., 165
Williamson, Harold F., Jr., 160
Wilson, James Q., 26, 91, 155, 163
Wilson, Robert L., 162
Wingo, Lowdon, 58, 59, 155, 157, 158, 159
Wisconsin, 23-24

Ylvisaker, Paul, 126, 165

Zoning, 101, 105-108, 112-113
Zuiches, James, 23, 25, 154

About the Author

Niles M. Hansen is Professor of Economics and Director, Center for Economic Development, at the University of Texas. He is the author of *French Regional Planning, France in the Modern World, Rural Poverty and the Urban Crisis, Intermediate-Size Cities as Growth Centers, Location Preferences, Migration and Regional Growth,* and *The Future of Nonmetropolitan America;* and the editor of *Growth Centers in Regional Economic Development* and *Public Policy and Regional Economic Development: The Experience of Nine Western Countries.* He also has contributed numerous articles to professional journals in economics and the social sciences.